Defying Discord

Ending the divide between your faith and "secular" art career

Marlita Hill

KAIIFA
PRESS

Published in Los Angeles, California, by Kaiifa Press.

Kaiifa Press titles may be purchased in bulk for educational purposes. For information, please email kaiifapress@gmail.com

Cover Design and Illustration by Jessie Nilo Design + Illustration
Illustrations by Hannah Sulak
Section Lettering Art by Raelyn Harrison, The Lettering Wall

ISBN: 978-0-692-88333-4

Printed in the United States

CONTENTS

ACKNOWLEDGEMENTS

Gosh, there are so many people to thank! Of course, I first want to thank God for trusting me with this assignment. Thank you to my family for their love and support. I want to honor my covering, Bishop Clarence and First Lady Priscilla McClendon, and the Full Harvest, International family. I want to give a humongous thank you to all the incredible artists I've met over the years—those who've shared their experiences, let me interview them, read my work, and listened to my talks and given feedback. Without your willingness to engage with me, this work wouldn't be what it is. Thank you to my visual collaborators: Hannah Sulak for your amazing illustrations, Jessie Nilo for that incredible book cover and graphic design, and Raelyn Harrison for your beautiful lettering art. A huge, huge thank you to my launch team who helped me get this book off the ground (Fallynne, Amy, Kristin, Clayton, Robin, Lauren, Nycole, Guy, Pastor Hoss, and Stefn). You guys are amazing!!! Another huge thank you to Arianna Caligiuri and the Edge Project Board and family for supporting me in developing this work, and for giving me an amazing opportunity in Spain to share and finish this work. Thank you to all my new Spain family. I'm so excited I get to come and spend life with you every summer. Diego Coello Fotógrafo, L'Interdit, Xef Pirata, Mama Rosa, Altea Arte, La Greda, and QVO: thank you for feeding me, teaching me some Spanish, and for your wonderful friendship. Liesel, Steve, and the Tolbert family, thank you for housing me during my transitional periods. I got a lot of writing done and was able to finish this work because you were so generous with your space. Pastor Hoss and Pastor Gerry, thank you for all that you did to help me make sure I wasn't saying anything crazy. Lastly, but most tremendously, Pastor Hoss: how can I ever begin to say Thank you—for your friendship, your guidance, your support, and so much more. I would not have made it through this transition without you. I know you're shy about being acknowledged but you will never know how much your presence has meant to me, my friends and fellow artists. We are all so blessed to have you in our corner. Thank you for being such a wonderful friend and man of God.

PREFACE

In the summer of 2017, I went on a trip to Sweden with my friend, Megan. When we arrived at the airport, we had to purchase our bus tickets to Linköping. On the way to the ticket counter, we passed by one of those airport stores. As I glanced into it, a book jumped out at me from the back wall. After we bought our tickets, we had ten minutes before the bus arrived and Megan wanted to grab some snacks. I thought, *Great*, and I made a bee-line to that book. The book was *Talk Like Ted*, by Carmine Gallo. We had a two-hour bus ride to Linköping, so I cracked it open as soon as I was settled in my seat.

In the first chapter, Gallo said this about working with clients: "In the early stages of building a story, I don't care about the product as much as I care about why the speaker is fired up about the product or service." He went on to give examples including Starbucks founder, Howard Schultz, who he said sells coffee, but is passionate about "building a third place between home and work..." He also mentioned Zappo's creator, Tony Hsieh, who sells shoes, but is passionate about "delivering happiness." Then Gallo writes, "Asking yourself, 'What's my product?' isn't nearly as effective as asking yourself, 'What business am I really in? What am I truly passionate about?'"

As I read that, I put my head back in my seat as I felt compelled to ask myself this very question: *What am I really passionate about?* I know what I'm teaching: how to get your faith, art, and career working together in harmony. I know who I'm talking to: Christians with "secular" art careers. But, what am I really after in doing this? What am I really hoping to occur once artists hear this teaching? And then it hit me, right there, in my seat on the Swebus, on the way to Linköping, Sweden.

I am passionate about liberty!

I've always been passionate about liberty; about artists being free to do whatever they feel God drawing them to do: however it looks, whatever it explores, wherever it exists, with whomever it involves. I'm passionate about artists seizing the art life God is leading them to build, without apology.

And yet, the sad reality is this: though so many artists feel drawn to be a Kingdom presence in "secular" culture through their careers, so few of them feel liberated to do so.

This is what I'm working to change.

There is a larger conversation about the Christian and their art, and about the Christian and their art taking space in the marketplace. This book occupies a specific place in that conversation. Structured as one unfolding chat between friends, this work takes a deep-dive approach to unpacking a single question: How do you serve God working out there, making that kind of art with those people? I've written from the conviction that this single question, this single unanswered, or wrongly answered, question lies at the root of this discord I confront in the title.

I mentioned my passion was liberty, and Defying Discord works to release these artists into the "free from" form of it. My assignment is to help them understand God wants them to be free from the burden of having to apologize for, justify, alter, diminish, feel guilty about, or choose between their faith and art career in "secular" culture, between honoring God and making "that kind" of art.

Thus, this is not a how-to book, which is about guidance on how to change something from what it is into something else. Instead, this is a how-does book, which is about affirming artists in Christ right in the location, expression, and associations their creative lives occupy.

This is a deep subject. It is a subject fraught with fear, misunderstanding, hurtful interactions, self-doubt, and isolation. Thus, it is a subject that must be tackled in an environment of absolute safety—of no judgment and brutal honesty, self-reflection and acknowledgment, of forgiveness and moving forward. What else embodies that safety but the company of a good friend.

So, to create this safe space, I've replaced all possible formality with familiarity, including my decisions to go against conventions of grammar, structure, and formatting. My word choices, the structure of my sentences and paragraphs, the layout and alignment of the text, even the non-conformity of the chapters, all serve to evoke the easygoing, laid-back comfort of talking to a good friend on a great couch—the perfect place for deep, soulful conversations about vulnerable matters of the heart...

the deep, rowdy, best-friend-type conversation that happens when you're kickin' it at the house, having great food, with all of the trespasses on proper etiquette and grammar that allows.

What do you experience as an artist in Christ, working in "secular" culture?

In my question, I'm not asking what people say about you being one.
I'm asking what you experience.
Inside.

INTRODUCTION

I was invited to lead a session at a worship arts retreat. After the session, a young man caught up with me as I was walking over to the dining hall. Let's call him Michael. Michael is a hip-hop dancer. He told me how much he enjoyed the session and began to share about his love for dance. He feels so alive in the pure adrenaline of taking class and working hard on new steps and combinations. But he feels guilty for enjoying it so much because he doesn't understand how taking a Hip-Hop class glorifies God. And if it doesn't glorify God, he doesn't know if it's something he should be doing, let alone enjoying.

I met another artist who loves fantasy gaming. Let's call her Amy. Amy and I were having a conversation while enjoying the sun on a beautiful terrace in Spain after a session I'd taught. As we were talking, she began telling me about this fantasy world she started designing for Dungeons and Dragons. She told me how she loved being a Dungeon Master, and that she wanted to design the worlds and environments for fantasy games. She actually wants to create a video game franchise! Fascinated, I asked Amy what she was doing to work toward it. I asked her when she was going to finish the game world she had started. She went on to tell me that she'd stopped designing it because she was conflicted about being a Christian in fantasy gaming. She knew about other Christians who had ventured in fantasy, like Lewis and Tolkien; but she wanted to work in a different facet of the genre. She didn't see how her faith could be integrated with the type of gaming she liked in a way that would be acceptable for a Christian. Since she couldn't imagine how they could coexist, she stopped. She didn't want to dishonor God.

I could tell you about many other artists I've met who share similar stories and battle similar dilemmas. What do they all have in common?

None of them yet feel truly liberated to just be the artist they feel drawn to be.
They all love God and want to live honorably before Him.
They're all artists with (or pursuing) careers in "secular" culture.

They're Christian, but they don't make art about faith or the Christian walk; nor is their art created to be used for evangelism, doctrine, or leading people in worship.

And because of this,
they struggle with the place of their art life in their faith walk.
They wrestle with the disconnection they believe exists between their faith, career, and artistry.
And, they're wondering if these three can actually live and thrive in the same space. And if so, how?

I asked you about your experience. If you're where I suspect, you, too, are wrestling in some way with the relationship between your faith and "secular" art career.

If that's true, I'm way too excited about the opportunity to encourage you.
I'm downright giddy that I get to let you know that is not the experience you should be having.
Yes, I know where you work.
I know the kind of art you create.
I know who you work with.
And yes, I'm aware of the absence of Christian reference and vocabulary in your work.
Still...
that's not the experience you should be having.

Let me tell you why.

When addressing the seven things the Lord hates and finds abominable, Proverbs 6:19 lists one of them as being "he who sows discord among his brethren." This phrase jumps out at me: *discord among his brethren*. The term, *brethren*, speaks to related parts, things in relationship, things related to one another, sharing the same parentage and origin.
As an artist in Christ working in "secular" culture, Christian, creative, and cultural participant are each a part of you that are related to one

another within you. Not only are they related, but they originate from the same Source.

You are a Christian, an identity He gave you through relationship with Him.

You create art, a gift and ability He gave you.

You work in "secular" culture, a context into which He drew you.

All aspects of your life, as an artist in Christ working in "secular" culture, have an origin and initiation in Him, and by Him. If that's really true, and it is, then they do not exist in conflict. If they're not in conflict, you shouldn't feel conflicted about being all three of them at the same time, in the same space.

So, why do you feel conflicted?

That's what we're going to tackle in the conversation that follows.

This book is part of a larger discipleship program I've created called the Kingdom Artist Initiative (KAI). The mission of my work is to help you become unapologetic about your "secular" art career.

Not disrespectful.

Not dishonorable.

Not without accountability.

Unapologetic.

What do I mean by that?

Well, on a basic level, I mean being in a place where you don't feel the need to justify or apologize for the kind of art you make, who you make it with, or where it lives.

But on a deeper level, I mean being unapologetic as a Christian having this kind of career, working in this context, intimately with "those" people.

How does one get there?

One, by being able to account for where God is, and is at work, in your career life.

And, two, by understanding how your kind of art career is a valid, God-honoring way to participate in Kingdom citizenship, building, and representation.

See, you don't have to apologize if you know that your art is for your life, not just your Christian service.

You don't have to apologize if you know that your art life has relevance, how it's relevant, that it makes a contribution, and what its contribution to the Kingdom is.

And, you don't have to apologize for your art career if you know it, too, has a place in Christian community and Kingdom purpose.

Now, we're going to tackle all of this through the KAI Freedom Formula:

Liberty + Harmony = an art life without apology

Basically, you have to be freed from some things.
You have to be rooted in some things.
And, you have to know how to walk in some things.

This is a conversation about you, my friend. So, be ready to chime in, push back, and give an answer.

Well, let's get to it.

In Our Defense

This whole idea of being unapologetic stands possible on one conviction: that any art life can be a vessel for worship, serve God, and leave a Kingdom footprint in culture.

Yes. You've read correctly.

ANY art life…no matter what you make art about, who you make it with, or where it lives.

ANY…

Now, I know what you're thinking.

At least, I think I know what you're thinking: *How is that even possible?*

Well, let's answer that by first looking at why you think it's not possible. Let's look at why we feel the need to be apologetic about our "secular" art careers at all.

Why does anyone feel the need to apologize?

Essentially, one apologizes as an acknowledgement that they've wronged someone, or committed some improper act.

I have two questions in response to that:

1) Where have Christians with "secular" art careers gotten the idea that what they're doing is wrong or improper?
2) What wrong are they supposedly doing that would need apology?

According to whom?

I believe there are several players that contribute to this narrative, but the root lies with one. Unfortunately, it's the church.

Let me explain what I mean.

As religion has grappled with the place of believers in culture, it hasn't always had the most gracious, informed, or at times, even Spirit-led response. The Spirit of God draws us out into culture. Yet, religion says if you're truly His, your life and art belong in the church, and to the church; and oh, by the way, here are the only acceptable ways to use your art here. There's an institutional fear of contamination and dilution; a deep-rooted, inherited legacy of dividing "sacred" and "secular" that has left many Christians ignorant about how to live out their faith in their everyday lives among people who are different than them. From that place of fear and dividedness, religion has marked out a very narrow set of acceptable ways to engage in faith, and in culture.

Our spiritual upbringing has made tension the default mode of interaction between our faith, our gifting, and the culture in which we live.

Even in churches where this isn't an issue, the residue of that mindset excludes discussion about life beyond the church service from most of the conversation happening within the church. It's relegated to the fringes, leaving scores of Christians who never hear anyone talk about engaging in "secular" culture in a spiritual and favorable way. Still, even when Christians are encouraged to seize their ambassadorship in culture, they're rarely taught how to actually do it. This is problematic because our church experience heavily forms the norms and mindsets we carry into our individual Christian walk. In essence, our spiritual upbringing has made tension the default mode of interaction between our faith, our gifting, and the culture in which we live.

That's where the thinking comes from. Now, what are the wrongs such artists are supposedly committing?

But, what did I do?

In answering that, let's look again at the artists our conversation is referencing:

They don't make art about faith or the Christian walk.

Their art is not created to be used for evangelism, doctrine, or leading people in worship.

They work closely with non-Christians.

Their art explores subjects that would most likely be deemed unacceptable in the local church.

They may even use bad language and their work is not always positive.

So, what are their offenses?

Well, according to the above mindset, they're the following:

Such an art life doesn't fulfill our Christian responsibility to worship, honor, and glorify God. Nor does it build the Kingdom.

Such an art life compromises the Christian, who will inevitably fall into darkness by association.

Such an art life taints God's pure and holy creation by mixing it in that world, with those people.

Such an art life betrays God's goodness to us by taking His gifts and using them for any other purpose than serving Him.

How'd I get pulled into this?

Now, I understand this is how our "secular" art careers can be perceived. But, how have we, as artists, gotten sucked up into that perception?

How has it happened in your life?

How do you,

who, in your quiet time, so powerfully sense God drawing you further into the art path you're on,

get caught up feeling guilty and conflicted about what you know is true?

I have a theory.

You get caught up because you're not confident that what you sense is, in fact, true, and truly from God. And you're not confident because you can't answer for it.

We're compelled to start moving forward in our art careers; yet, we get sucked up in this insanity because of guilt. Oftentimes, we're the only ones in our immediate circle feeling drawn to take this path with our art. Or, we think we're the only one because no one's talking about it. It's like people are doing it, but everyone's in the closet about it. And since they're in the closet, it seems there's nowhere to go with what we're experiencing. We feel alone in these feelings we're feeling, in these thoughts we're having, in this drawing compelling us to go into that world with those people to engage in this work.

And since we seem to be the only one afflicted by this compulsion, we start to wonder if we actually heard God? We start to wonder if He would actually lead us to do what we're feeling led to do.
No one else around us seems to be struggling with this.
No one else even seems to be considering it.
No one's really talking about it; and if they do, it's rarely positive.

Is there something wrong with us for pursuing what we're pursuing?
For wanting it?
And yet, the drawing doesn't stop.
The intensity doesn't let up.
The visions remain vivid.
Our heart is still lit afire whenever we think about it.

In this back and forth, we're weighted down with uncertainty, which leads to conflict. That only adds to the struggle because we're unsure if this is something we have the right to be conflicted about. Should we even be considering this?

And *that* back and forth gives way to guilt.

You see, the guilt, the inability to stand unapologetically in our art career, comes from the inability to provide any answer for it.

We don't know how to answer for what we're being drawn to pursue.

We don't know how to explain why it makes perfect Kingdom sense that we would live for God by pouring that life into something that doesn't seem to acknowledge or tend to Him at all.

We don't know how to show that it's actually all about Him, rooted in Him, initiated by Him; even though it doesn't fit the larger, but narrow, understanding of what being for Him looks like.

We don't know how to defend the way He's at work in what we're doing.

But we're in a conversation about embracing this career life without apology. We're talking about creating free from conflict, unencumbered by guilt. That's only made possible by what you know.

So, what do you need to know to thrive in your "secular" art career without apology?

1 Ptr. 3:15-16 says,
> "But sanctify the Lord God in your hearts, and always *be* ready to *give* a defense to everyone who asks you a <u>reason for the hope</u> that is in you, with meekness and fear; <u>having a good conscience</u>, that when they defame you as evildoers, those who revile <u>your good conduct in Christ</u> may be ashamed."

First of all, you need to know why you're hoping for the things you're hoping for. You need to know that this artistic hope you carry is a Godly hope. It's there because God put it there. And you're going after it because He's compelled you to pursue it.

Second, you need to know you're entitled to a good conscience about your career. A conscience is good and clear because it knows that what it's involved in is good. You have a right to a good conscience about your "secular" art career because it's God's work in you. It's a part of His promise for your life.

Third, you need to know that your art career is regarded as good conduct in Him.

Yes, even your kind of career.

How?

The career you're forging is based on a vision He planted in you. It's based on directions He gave you. It's inspiration born out of prayer and seeking Him. When He answered, you moved on the answer. That's faith.

That's obedience.

That's honor and worship.

As you pursue your career, God sees you exercising belief in Him.

He looks at that and says it is GOOD!

That's not all you need to know, though.

Being able to stand unapologetically in your art career requires more than just knowing these things. It requires you to be convinced about them. And that comes from understanding *how* they're true.

Our freedom formula says liberty + harmony = an art life without apology. Liberty comes through a root transfer, where we remove the erroneous, misplaced things we've learned, experienced, observed, and accepted; while planting new roots of truth about being an artist in Christ.

I want to perform this root transfer by debunking those four "offenses" we spoke about earlier. Let's start with the biggest one: Such an art life doesn't fulfill our Christian responsibility to worship, honor, and glorify God. Nor does it build the Kingdom.

Liberty
+
harmony
=

an art life
with apology

2 A Part, My Part

We've made it clear the kind of artists we're talking about. How does one honor, serve, and glorify God in that kind of career, making that kind of art?

This is a very important question. In fact, the inability to answer this question makes it very difficult to be a confident artist in Christ, and stand in the validity of one's art career.

As Christians with "secular" art careers, we don't always feel comfortable with the idea that our kind of art life is honorable before God, that it's worthy of acceptance in our faith walk, or that it contributes any value to the Kingdom.

So, let's just shut that foolishness down right now.

The thing to remember is that, within us, faith, art, and career all come from the same parent.
We're in relationship with God because He initiated the relationship.
We have artistic gifts and inclinations because that's how He built us.
We create the kind of art we create about the kind of subjects we explore because that's where He inspires us.
And, we're compelled to a career in "secular" culture because that's the context into which He's drawn us.

If it's initiated, formed, and led by Him, how could our art life not honor Him or contribute to His Kingdom?

Where, then, does this line of thinking even come from?

I'm going to highlight two contributors: our tendency to reduce our relationship with God to being useful, and our method misplacement.

The Usefulness Obsession

In the local church, there's generally a four-pronged focus: evangelism, worship, spiritual growth, and day-to-day business and operations. Only things that serve those priorities are accepted easily. If an element falls outside of them, the church, generally, has no infrastructure to deal with it. I'm sure you've experienced some form of this as an artist who doesn't use their art for any of these four purposes.

Where, then, do you fit in that church?
And if you don't fit in the church, where do you fit in the Kingdom?
Since we're not directly useful to their priorities, it can feel like the church is against us. But, are they?
Most likely not.

There are denominations and churches that still believe Christians should have no dealings with "secular" society; but I find it hard to believe that you'd attend such a church in the first place. The more likely case is that they just don't know what to do with you. What you do doesn't fall within their areas of focus.

In addition to this, we have this tendency to reduce our relationship with God, and our value to Him in that relationship, to how useful we are to Him. Since we struggle to imagine how our kind of art career could possibly be useful to God, we fall into believing that our career has no place in our faith life.

So, the church influences our individual spiritual walk.
They have specific priorities, and are partial to things that directly serve those priorities.
(By the way, I'm not saying there's anything at all wrong with that. In fact, I think it's prudent.)
But...

If they're focused on things that directly serve their priorities, to the oversight of those that don't, what narrative do you think is being formed in us about our art career, if they're our spiritual model?

If our art and career don't fit into the priorities of the model we pattern ourselves after, what place do they have in our lives?

Thus, the usefulness struggle with our art careers.

You see, we equate church priorities, and their way of doing ministry, as the only possible way to participate in Kingdom enterprise.
And, that's just not the case.
The local church has its part to play in the Kingdom, and we have ours.
They have their way of participating, and we have ours.
Unfortunately, with our part being pushed to the fringes, if included at all, we're both often inadequate at explaining what our part is, and what it looks like. Beyond evangelism, we both struggle to articulate why artists in Christ are being drawn to "secular" culture, or how their presence serves the Kingdom there.

In my opinion, I feel like we just need to get out from under the ludicrousness of usefulness altogether.

Why?

Because God is not in relationship with you because you're useful to Him. He's not in relationship with you because your gift is useful to Him. He's in relationship with you because He's in love with you; and He's gifted you as an expression of that love.

Bottom line.

In Eph. 3:17-19, Paul prays "that Christ may dwell in [our] hearts through faith; that [we], being rooted and grounded in love, may be able to comprehend with all the saints what *is* the width and length and depth and height— to know the love of Christ which passes knowledge; that [we] may be filled with all the fullness of God."

He doesn't pray that we come to know all the ways Christ wants to use us.

I understand that our Kingdom citizenship involves putting our lives, gifts, faculties, and resources to use in building and furthering the Kingdom. I also understand that part of that is done by using them to help the local church fulfill its part. However, I'm also very aware of our tendency to quickly turn service into exploitation and manipulation; leaving people thinking that the only good they're for is to be used. Have you ever experienced that?

Well, believe it or not, your artistry and career are for more than just service.

> ## Your art is not just something you use in Christian service or for your career. Your art is part of how God has given you to engage during your time in this earth.

Communion

A father gives his son a fishing pole so they can go to the lake and spend time together as they fish. In the same way, your art life is a way for you and God to spend life together, learning more about each other over shared activity. Intimacy is forged in communal experiences. In close proximity, focused on the same things, common ground is found. Mutual language is developed. Mutual experience is discovered. At some point, a shift happens where you no longer come together for the activity, but the activity serves as a way to be together.

My own relationship with God has deepened so much through my art practice. He's taught me a lot over dance: about Him, about me, about life.

I've learned how He works, as we've walked together through all the processes, projects, and pursuits I've navigated as a dancer.

I've learned how He sees me, as He's encouraged me through the bumps, bruises, setbacks, failures, and disappointments that come with being a career artist.

In many ways, I feel closest to Him when I'm teaching, taking class, or choreographing; when I'm doing what He built me to do. Throughout the ups and downs of career life, we build trust, understanding, and intimacy. I make myself vulnerable to Him as I lean into Him, and invite Him into my creative practice and ambition. And He ministers His goodness, partnership, creativity, provision and guidance to me.

Formation

One day, I was sitting in my house and the Lord brought up the image of a potter handling clay (Jer 18:6 / Isa 64:8). He asked me, *Does a potter form clay in stillness?* I thought about it and answered, *No.* He then began to minister to me how He forms us in our pursuit. Just like clay is put into motion, and formed while in motion, so are we by the dreams and desires God agitates us to pursue.
There are issues that will never surface,
people we'll never meet,
questions that will never arise,
circumstances we'll never encounter,
qualities and capacities we'll never discover,
emotions that we'll never experience while we're standing still.
They only show themselves as we attempt, and face, situations and people in our career pursuit.

God, in His infinite wisdom, uses these encounters to smooth, remove, mature, build up, and fortify us into that divine fitness we're told about in 2 Tim. 3:17. As we pursue, He has us on His wheel; His hands working on our character, our worldview, our heart, and even refining our desire and ambition.

As we move out on things we believe God is directing, He refines our ability to discern His voice and leading.

As we go after the things we think we want, He refines our desires as we discover what is, and isn't, substantive and truly fulfilling.

As we take opportunities, He refines our values as we discover the kinds of things that really matter about having, opportunity, and accomplishment.

As we interact with people, He refines our character as we learn how to be treated, and how to treat others as those for whom God also cares.

In pursuit, we develop those character muscles that really make it possible to follow God all the way into our promise, like knowing how to wait, persevere, and overcome. It's not until you have to wait that you learn how to wait. These are things that are formed and sharpened by use.

Instruction

Do you ever wonder why Jesus taught so much through parables? And why those parables always seemed to be about birds, plants, vineyards, trees, landowners, and fields?

Well, a parable is an instructional tool and strategy. In them, you put two things alongside one another for the sake of comparison, so that key concepts can be learned by the comparison. Jesus was masterful at this. He put spiritual truth alongside stories of things that were familiar to His listeners. Through the stories, they were able to take what they knew about the subject to help them understand the spiritual concept. Jesus' parables were often about birds, plants, and vineyards because these were things His listeners encountered every day. They were a part of how they lived.

In education, we call this accessing prior knowledge: I take what you already know and use it to help you understand what I'm trying to teach you right now. In the same way, the Holy Spirit will teach you spiritual truth through stories and examples using your art life. You see, art is also your lens and language for understanding spiritual truth. Just like Jesus taught agricultural people using agricultural terms and processes, He'll do the same thing with you in artistic terms. He'll use the vernacular, processes, and culture of what you know to help you understand Him more deeply.

Service

Your gift and career are also for service. You are absolutely supposed to put them to use to build and advance God's people and His kingdom. But you are not God's tool. He doesn't sweep you back and forth to clean up the dirtiness of His earth. He doesn't bang you against wood and nails to build His walls. The service you do for God is to be done in the environment of communion, in the context of a loving relationship, out of a heart of gratitude and reciprocity for all His goodness toward you.

You are not God's Cinderella. He does not use you. To use you means that He's willing to sacrifice your well-being for His purpose; which He is not willing to do.

Instead, the two of you, as co-laborers in a loving relationship, put to use what He's given you in the stewardship of His purposes.

Anchoring (Healing and Processing)

My family has had its rough patches. Some were definitely rougher than others. In that, I got lost in the shuffle and fell into a struggle with pornography. Can I tell you that God met me in that struggle on the dance floor? I remember the height of it was during my time ministering with The Hush Company, which was a dance ministry in Los Angeles, directed by Stacy Meadows and LaQuin Snowden. I was struggling with porn while I was travelling around the country ministering to God's people. And He never once condemned me for it. He never spoke to Stacy and LaQuin and told them to remove me from the group. Instead, He used dance to anchor me to Himself as He healed all the things in my heart that left me prey, and made me want to run to porn to find any kind of relief and escape.

Dance was a way for me to process and release. There were times when I was so angry, so lonely, so hurt that I would dance like my life depended on it. Sometimes, I would dance so hard that my back would shake violently and my chest would burn after we were done. There were times where I would completely ignore the people because I was reaching with everything in me for every ounce of deliverance for myself.

Dance was the only place I could go and feel like I was truly heard. I didn't always have the words to express how I felt, nor the confidence to say them when I found them. But I knew how to take it into the movement, and I knew how to leave it all on the floor. It was my prayer. It was my cry out to God. And He was always faithful to meet me there. It's always been our secret place where I could scream out and not have to explain or justify myself. I could just release and receive.

Most importantly, dance has been a way for me to move forward. He's used it to pull me through many rough patches in my life. He does it by filling me with His vision for me as an artist. He does it by filling my heart with overwhelming joy whenever I do it. He uses it to fill me with hope, taking me beyond things I'm fighting against by giving me things to fight for. He's uses dance to root me in value and identity as He teaches me more about who I am, what I have to contribute, and what He's excited to do in partnership with me.
The same is available for you.
Sometimes, we feel guilty about wanting to run to our art instead of running to God.
Don't!
Run to it, and He'll meet you there.

Enjoyment

Your art and career are also for you to enjoy. 1 Tim. 6:17 tells us that God "gives us richly all things to enjoy."
Not to serve Him with, but to enjoy.
For *you* to enjoy, not just someone else.

Why are we so reticent, so hesitant, so afraid to simply enjoy God's goodness to us? I like to use real examples, so, to me, it's like sex. We struggle with simply enjoying sex, or talking about sex as something that can be simply enjoyed. It's a gift from God. Yes, it's for procreation. Yes, it's a way for man and wife to grow closer to one another.
But, y'all let's live a little...it's also for fun.
Sex is fun!
Why are we so afraid to admit that and embrace it? Why can't we just admit that it feels really good and we have an amazing time doing it? Why are we acting like God, Himself, didn't build our anatomy to capture and experience the amazing sensations sex provides?

Like sex, our artistry is a gift that, in addition to service, is also meant to simply be enjoyed.

God gave you art and creativity because He wants you to experience the joy that comes from experiencing, making, and sharing it. Jesus said He came to give us life more abundantly. Well, life more abundantly has to be more than just life for service.
Think about marriage.
If marriage was nothing else, literally nothing else, but cleaning up after someone, who would want to do it? If you experienced no enjoyment, received no emotional or relational reward from it,
if it was nothing but duty and service,
why would anyone do that...willingly?

Marriages need time for enjoyment. Think about what happens when that very important element is neglected. Think about how difficult even sex becomes when it's reduced to getting pregnant. That relationship suffers when no opportunity is given for sex simply to enjoy one another.

If you're not enjoying your life in art, you're not experiencing the full benefit of being an artist in relationship with God.

Consider this:
You're not in relationship with God.
I mean, yes, He's God. But to you and I, He's Daddy.
We're in relationship with Daddy; and our Daddy happens to be God.
It's like if your dad was Jason Statham.
To you, he's dad; it's just that your dad happens to be the BADDEST dude on the planet.
But you don't interact with him as Jason Statham, BADDEST dude on the planet.
You interact with him as Dad.

Since God is our Dad, tell me: What healthy, loving father doesn't want their child to experience joy, fulfillment, and happiness? And not just experience it, but have a life full of it? God is the same way. Yes, He's God. But to you and I, He's Daddy. And healthy daddies want their children happy. This is why it's important to remember who we're in relationship with when we think about our art life in Christ.

Like Michael, who felt guilty for being edified and enlivened through Hip-Hop class, we often struggle with guilt because of how good doing art makes us feel.
Please don't!
Like any parent who gives a gift to their child, watching you shamelessly, unapologetically enjoy what He's given you is one of His greatest rewards.

Method Misplacement

Before we go on, let's remember the issue we're addressing. It's believed that our "secular" art career fails to honor God and build the Kingdom.

We said this thinking comes from two things. One is our tendency to reduce our relationship with God to being useful, which we just addressed. The other is method misplacement.

What is that?

Basically, it's what's happening when a kidney tries to tell a patella (knee-cap) how it should function based on how the kidney functions in its context.

I know, it sounds crazy. Let me explain.

In 1 Cor. 12, Paul uses the human body as a powerful analogy for the diversity in the body of Christ. He's specifically talking about spiritual gifts as manifestations of the Spirit. However, there's a larger principle that we can apply to our conversation.

Essentially, there are different gifts; and each of these gifts have a specific mix of particulars that impact the way the gift functions. Even when you have multiple people with the same gift, these particulars cause them to be used in very different ways. Not every singer sings to the exact same audience, or composes in the exact same genre. Not every person who can sing uses their gift to sing. Some singers pursue large audiences, while others prefer coffee houses. Some use their gift to perform, while others use theirs in education or therapy.

The important point that Paul is making is that this diversity exists on purpose, and serves the same purpose. Regardless of where it's used, how it's used, or who it's used to serve, the gifts come from the same source, and they're being directed by that same source.

Also, each of these gifts have a different environment which requires a specific way of governance. The management of a gift in one environment is different than the management of that gift in another. But it's the same God managing both gifts. And, both gifts are contributing to the same larger purpose. If that's the case, the difference in use and management is not dishonoring to God; and it still serves Him even though it's different. If we don't recognize this, we end up trying to apply modes of governance in environments for which they're not suited.

We see this play out between Peter and Paul.

Basically, these two get into a dispute over the path for justification (Gal. 2). Peter says the path must include circumcision. Paul says it absolutely does not. It only requires faith in the Lordship of Jesus Christ. In such a dispute, we usually focus on trying to figure out who's wrong.

Neither of them are. Well, almost.

But before we get into that, here we're dealing with two men engaging with the same concept from two different contexts. Both of them are dealing with justification. Yet, they were sent to communicate the same gospel to two different groups of people who existed in very different circumstances. These circumstances affected how each man spoke about the gospel to their group.

First, you have Peter: the apostle to the Jews. The Jews had been observing the law since it was instituted through Moses. Circumcision was a part of that law. The law absolutely had a purpose in God's plan for their justification; but it's purpose was only to bring them to Christ. It was never meant to be a path to justification, in itself. Now that Christ is here, the law is no longer needed. But it's been such a part of their life for so long, they choose to continue observing it, even though they no longer need to. In communicating the gospel to them, then, Peter speaks to them from this place. He knows they no longer need to observe it. But they've chosen to stay under the law, so he speaks to them from that place in order to bring them to Christ. Therefore, circumcision is a regular part of their conversation.

Paul, on the other hand, is the apostle to the Gentiles. The Gentiles have never had to observe the law, as it was specifically for the Jews, whom God separated for Himself until the time of Christ when all people would have access to Him through salvation. The Gentiles have never learned the law. They've never had to be circumcised, observe feasts and seasons, offer specific sacrifices – they've never had to do any of that. All they've ever known is that faith in the Lordship of Jesus Christ is all that's needed for justification. So, in communicating the gospel to them, circumcision has no place in their conversation.

This dispute between Peter and Paul happens because Peter tries to impose his context onto people who are not in his context. Basically, Peter was a kidney trying to tell patellas how they should function based on how kidneys function.

How does this apply to our conversation?

In terms of this whole issue of honoring God and building the Kingdom, I'm proposing that we, as Christians with "secular" art careers, are caught in this same kidney/patella dilemma. Who tells us (or leaves us to believe) that our kind of art lives fail to honor and serve? They're people who are working toward the same end, but are pursuing that end from within a different context. To them, our art lives fall short because our method is different. Our path to that same end looks different because our context is different.

Like the dispute between Peter and Paul, we scramble trying to figure out who's wrong; which is missing the point entirely. Part of the liberty in Christ is that we are free to engage the gospel through the particulars of our specific context. It's not about whether the kidneys or the patellas are doing it right. It's that they've been given different ways to do it in the first place. Therefore, kidneys need to stay in the kidney lane, and let patellas do things the way it's needed for their lane.

The opinion is that our kind of art career does not honor, glorify and worship God, or build the Kingdom. We also get pinned with this question: "But what is your ministry?"

What do these even mean?

Honor
By 1 Sam. 2:29 and Isa. 58:13, we find that honor is a way of responding to God because of how you see Him; because of the esteem in which you hold Him. Out of this esteem comes the conviction that He deserves the best of whatever He requests. It's also the resolve that you will bring Him your best. Materially, it's the best of your substance and resource. Spiritually, it's pressing beyond your own ways, pleasures, and opinions to do your best in obeying Him to the fullest extent possible. Gift-wise, it's offering the best version of your gift to be utilized however He sees fit. Honor is about the kind of response you give, and the quality of what you bring in that response, because of how you see Him.

Glorify
In John 17, Jesus gives us insight into what it means to glorify God when He says, "I have glorified You on the earth. I have finished the work which You have given Me to do." 1 Cor 6:20 says, "For you were bought at a price; therefore glorify God in your body and in your spirit, which are God's."

To glorify God is to find what He has for you to do, and to use all that is in you, and at your disposal, to become and fulfill it.

Worship
Romans 12:1 tells us to present ourselves a living sacrifice, or a sacrifice that will live, holy and acceptable unto God which is our reasonable service, or worship. We worship God when we offer our lives to Him to be freely disposed to whatever place, to do whatever task, with whomever He needs. It's like going to a friend's house and saying, "I'm

here however you need me. Whatever you need me to do, just tell me and I'll do it."

Ministry

Contrary to popular belief, our ministry is not the position we hold in church, or even the tasks we do there. These are ways we fulfill our ministry, which is different. According to 2 Cor. 5:18-19, our actual ministry is reconciliation.

Reconciliation is about creation being back in relationship with God, which starts at salvation. But it's also about His creation being reconciled, or restored, back to the purpose, the quality, the wholeness, the potency, the proximity, and the order in which He first formed it.

Reconciliation is possibly God's highest priority. So, any directive He gives serves that purpose. That would mean that every time we follow His leading, we're participating in the ministry of reconciliation.

Now, these are simple definitions, and there's more nuance to each of them. However, I want you to notice something about them: they're anatomical definitions. We're told what they are, but not what they have to look like. There's no place where scripture tells us that any of these four practices can only be done in a certain way: i.e. in a certain place, with certain people, at a certain time, using certain things, etc.

In fact, what we find is that we're given room for, what I call, contextual practice, meaning we're free to engage in these four things in whatever way is suitable and appropriate for our particular context. This means that it's totally possible for one person to glorify God, and it look one way in that context; and for another to also glorify God in a separate context, and it look completely different.

In a KAI workshop, I asked the group this question: *What are the "acceptable" ways for a Christian to have an art career in "secular" culture (at least according to what you've been taught, told, or have experienced)?* Some of the answers were that the art include obvious Christian language with an obvious Christian message, that the art be made for Christian audiences, that it be family-friendly and avoid controversial subjects and language, that the business structure be non-profit, that the art have an evangelistic slant, and that it have a positive message.

This is what many of us hear our "secular" art careers look like. The problem is that it doesn't fit our context. Here's an analogy to demonstrate what I mean:

I was thinking about law enforcement employees. All of them are working to maintain law and order, and protect the public. Within the larger group of employees, there are subgroups. Each of the subgroups have different ways of achieving what they're all working to accomplish.

Group A consists of employees that strictly deal with other law enforcement employees, like HR, IAB, mental health support, etc. Everyone they serve already ascribes to the mission and works within that system. This group of employees serves the larger purpose by tending to the infrastructure, and to the groundworkers who need training, support, and accountability.

Group B is the groundworkers, the officers, who work out in the community with people who are not law enforcement. They're uniformed, making it obvious who they are and what they're about. They serve the larger mission of maintaining safety and order by making it obvious that law enforcement is present. But, their uniform only allows them to serve the larger mission to a certain extent, as it limits their access to certain spheres of people and activity. With their intentions and identity being obvious, it's easy for people who want to avoid them to do so.

This is where Group C, the undercover officers, are needed. There are crimes and criminals that will never be discovered while it's obvious that law enforcement is present. These officers are able to serve the larger mission in adverse environments by shielding their identity and intentions with commonality. Instead, their strategy bypasses the avoidance trigger by finding common ground, which leads to access. The access leads to relationship. The relationship provides them proximity so they can actually see where, and how, the law needs to be enforced when it's time.

As artists in Christ, we're like these law enforcement employees.
We're all serving the same mission.
All of us want to serve God with our gifts.
All of us want God to be honored and glorified by what we do with them.
All of us want to use our gifting to contribute to building the Kingdom.
All of us desire to see people reconciled to God and living in purpose.
Yet, we exist in three different contexts.

There's the to-the-church context, where the artist is working among people who already ascribe to the same mission, and exist within the same system. They already share a common language and hold the beliefs ascribed to by that language. Here the artist contributes to the spiritual infrastructure, helping the church-community engage with the gospel in corporate worship, ministering the word, spiritual formation, and fellowship.

There's the from-the-church context, where the artist goes out into the community to interact with people who don't necessarily ascribe to their mission. Their intentions for interacting with the community are focused and are made obvious. They serve the larger mission by sharing the gospel. They're successful with people who are mission-adjacent: who are either curious, receptive, or convinced and wanting further engagement. But their obviousness only allows them to serve the larger mission to a certain degree. It restricts their access to certain spheres of people and activity, making it easy for those who want to avoid them to do so.

And, there's the marketplace context. Here, it's about embodying the gospel. These artists serve the larger mission by doing their art. They're able to bypass avoidance triggers within "secular" society by establishing common ground as creative professionals. The common ground leads to access. The access leads to relationship. The relationship provides proximity. The proximity leads to permission. The permission opens the door to influence. The influence provides the privilege to speak and have your words be received with impact and consequence.

Same mission,
existing in different contexts,
which require different strategies of engagement.

Within these three contexts, there are two ways we participate in Kingdom citizenship as artists. There are two ways we approach "secular" society as Kingdom citizens. For artists in the to-the-church and from-the-church contexts, the prevalent strategy is verbal. Here, it's all about participating through your conversation and language. It's all about message.
How is the faith life being talked about?
Where is the message being spoken?
How is the doctrine being communicated?

Remember, these two contexts are mainly focused on tending the needs of the local church, which focuses on leading the congregation in worship, ministering the word, spiritual formation, and expanding the church through evangelism. All these are accomplished through message.

The marketplace context doesn't use message to engage. It doesn't approach "secular" society through message, either. Remember, for those of us in this context, we have to bypass that avoidance trigger. Christian language and vocabulary are like the officer's uniform. People can spot it a mile away, limiting our access to certain spheres who don't want to hear that message. So, our participation strategy cannot be the message spoken. Here, the strategy is embodiment. The faith life is embodied, then seen and observed through our lens, our practice, our character, and our interaction. That is, until we've established relationship and received permission to share the gospel in a life or environment.

What does this embodiment look like?

This is important information for you to know.
Why?
One of the reasons people dismiss your art career in Kingdom service is because they only know to look for the message.

3 Beyond the Talk

Al is a science fiction writer. He writes science fiction because he loves the form and conventions of the genre. His stories are not an allegory or metaphor about a Christian story or principle. He's not trying to address or comment on any social issue through a scriptural lens. He simply likes writing interesting science fiction. He writes for the sheer and singular joy of making art in this genre.

Jeanette is a concert musician who performs her own avant garde compositions for violin. Her work doesn't tackle social issues. She's not playing to help people experience healing through music, though music is a vehicle for healing. She doesn't compose from a narrative place. She's not trying to say or represent anything in her music, except that she enjoys the playful tension of string instrumentation freed from counts and metrical constraints.

If we were only using the message in Al's art to determine whether it could serve or represent the Kingdom, we would say that his art could do neither of those things. We would say it isn't Christian enough, that he's not representing the faith as much as he could. We would feel there aren't enough Christian references. We would ask him what's supposed to happen spiritually for people after reading his work.

If we're only focusing on the message in Jeanette's music, we wouldn't consider her expression to have a place in the Christian walk, either. And since it's not being used to produce any spiritual outcome, we wouldn't consider her work to be a good representation of a Christian artist using their art to serve God.

When the Lord gave me the Kingdom Artist Initiative (KAI), He was adamant that I use the wording, art life, not just art. This differentiation seems insignificant, but is actually worlds apart. Our quest in this book is that you be unapologetic about your "secular" art career. That's not possible unless you believe that any art life can serve, build, and represent the Kingdom.

And any can.

The reason any art life can serve and honor God is because you have a life in art, not just a message in art. And your life in art serves God and builds the Kingdom, even when the message in your art doesn't directly talk about it.

You see, if we just say art, and not art life, our only available means of transaction is through what our art says. But that's not the only way we can serve, communicate, honor, glorify, worship, represent, or demonstrate. And *that* reality requires a bigger container than just what our art says.

Now, let's look at this art life. It has three parts:

There's the person, which is who you are.
There's the process, which is how you do things.
And, there's the product, which is the art piece, and by extension, the message in the piece, if there even is a message.

PERSON

Before you ever put brush to paint, fingers to keys, character to plot, steps to music, you have to know that YOU are so much more than just an artist, though you are an artist fully and absolutely. As a member of the body of Christ, you are a person of tremendous consequence.

When people interact with you, an artist in Christ, a person bought by the blood and filled with the Spirit of God, they interact with a son of the Most High. When you step into a room, you, as a believer, carry something that impacts the environment of that room. When you interact with a life, you have the capacity to release that life into the wholeness God has made available to them. When you speak with someone, the words that come out of your mouth have weight and power.

Just by being present, *you* are a vessel for worship and *you* are leaving a Kingdom footprint in your environment. I love how my friend Tawanna coins this. She calls it the ministry of presence.

When I teach KAI workshops, I talk about how we participate in this ministry of presence by being salt, light, fragrance, and love.

Mt. 5:13 says you are the salt of the earth. You, with your presence, can stand in the gap and release the preserving power of God. You can salt the earth and stand against ungodly things that are trying to remain or reproduce. You can stimulate life in people, situations and environments. You carry the force of life that, when released, causes people to thrive.

Mt. 5:14 says you are the light of the world. As a son, all that is in you is full of light. God strategically puts you on display for His glory. When people see you, do they encounter one who emanates the glory, the goodness and the grace of God? Do they encounter one whose rootedness in Christ compels them to get closer and inquire about what makes you so different? Or do they encounter a self-centered, judgmental person emanating the condemnation of religion?

2 Cor. 2:14 says you release the fragrance of Christ. You give a picture of who God is, and what it's like to be in relationship with Him. For many people, the first perception they have of God will be formed by an encounter with you, His body and His representative. You hold the ability to show a God who lavishly loves on His children, engages Himself in their lives, and invests His whole being in their success, happiness, and wholeness. You, by the way you live in Him, have the ability to provoke hope in others to have the same relationship with their Creator, and thrive in the reason He brought them into this earth.

Finally, you are the exhibitor and dispenser of the love of God. By seeing and treating people as someone Christ died for, someone He felt was worth His own life, you can dignify and cultivate people into the greatness God intends for their life. You can love them into the fullness and wholeness He has made available to them.

Your art life can be a vessel for worship and leave a Kingdom footprint by who you determine to be as a person making art, beyond the kind of art you make. If you notice, the Bible says you *are* salt, light, fragrance, and love before you ever do, or make, anything. It's who you are. By simply being present, and releasing what you carry as He leads you, you can be an artist of great Kingdom impact. If you're able to embrace your saltiness, release your light and His fragrance, and walk in love, you can make art of any form, in any context and still have a career that glorifies Him.

But that's just part of it.

It starts in you

I attended a lecture about the intersection of faith and work. One of the attendees shared his dilemma as a software designer. His work mostly consists of writing code. The Lord has favored him and prospered his business. But he shared that he can't enjoy the success because he feels guilty as he doesn't see how building code at a desk is building the Kingdom.

Some might suggest that a remedy for his guilt can be found in refocusing his work, building software for churches, missional organizations, or other causes that serve Christian purposes.

I don't think that's necessary, unless God leads you to do that. Here's why:

Yes, we're supposed to build the Kingdom. But, the kingdom of God is in *you* (Lk 17:21). You see, most times, when we think about serving and building the Kingdom, we think about doing so externally: either by addition (adding people to the Kingdom by salvation) or service (involving ourselves in some organizational activity serving Kingdom priorities).

But the Kingdom of God is within you; and within you, there's Kingdom work to be done. Part of the Kingdom of God is His rule, or His divine influence on the way you see, do, and speak in your life. When you submit to God's divine influence over an area in your life, the Kingdom is expanded. And with every new area you submit to His influence, His Kingdom is expanded that much more. This continues until the Kingdom expands out of you, beyond you, into everything and everyone you come in contact with - until it reaches your family, your artistry, your career life, and your collaborations.

Serving the Kingdom starts within you because the Kingdom has its dwelling, operation, and expression in you...when you let it. We won't see the Kingdom of God externally manifested until there are people who allow the Kingdom of God to thrive within them internally, by submitting to the influence and leading of the Spirit of God.

So, despite what you make art about, you, in your person, serve and build the Kingdom as you participate in your conformation into Christ's image (Rom 8:29):
by renewing your mind,
redirecting your focus for living,
reconciling the various facets of your life,
and rehabilitating your conduct.

Working on yourself *is* serving the Kingdom. The more you die to yourself (mortify your flesh), the more room the Kingdom has to expand and operate within you, until it extends out of you and into your external environments, activities and interactions.

PROCESS

Your process is the way you manage and execute things in your art life.
How do you create art?
How do you make career and business decisions?
How do you go about executing them?
How do you interact with other people?
Even more practically, we're talking about the way you prepare to
compose, the way you negotiate business deals and pursue
opportunities, the way you deal with your dancers, etc.

How can the processes you use in your art life honor God, be a vessel
for worship and leave a Kingdom footprint in culture?

As we unpack this question, let's first look at it in terms of citizenship
and representation.

Citizenship

The reality of your Christian experience is that upon salvation, you
became a new creation,
were made a citizen of a new kingdom,
and you were made accountable to a new system.
This new system is governed by different laws,
it upholds different standards and values,
practices different customs,
and has a different way of getting things done.

Think about citizenship in its natural sense. As a citizen of the United
States of America, I have rights. But I'm also governed by a set of rules,
laws, and customs that inform the things I do and ways I participate as a
citizen. If I'm going to experience success, I need to learn and
cooperate with the rules, laws, and customs that govern this country. If
I move to another country, I have to let go of the U.S. system of

governance, and learn and cooperate with the new governance that exists where I now live.

In the Kingdom of God, righteousness is the system of governance (1 Jn. 3:7). One aspect of righteousness is that it's God's way of being and doing right; basically, doing things His way. This is a sacrifice as it involves killing your opinions and methods, and taking His on instead. Further, doing it His way requires an act of faith that His way will bring equal or better results than doing it your own way.

And that, in itself, is an act of worship.

Taking God at His word,
believing Him,
trusting Him,
and following Him are acts of worship.
Creating your art,
furthering your career,
and interacting with others, in the ways He's leading, is an act of worship.
It's an act of worship that can be lifted up to God as an R&B musician, an art director, a music video choreographer, a Baroque composer, etc. It builds the Kingdom, leaves its footprint, and has nothing to do with the message or usefulness of your art.

Representation

As a believer, you have two concurrent processes going on within you. There's an *in-you* process, and a *through-you* process.

The *in-you* process is at work to bring you into maturity and fruitfulness. It's to equip you so that you're fit for every good work.
It's to nourish you in all the identity and know-how you need to thrive and live in the quality of life God has made available to you.

In the *through-you* process, God takes that maturity, fruitfulness, and fitness, and puts it on display as the two of you collaborate in purpose. In this public display and collaboration, you become His walking Yelp review on what life with Him is like. This is important because it creates

When you allow Him to lead you, the Father can be glorified in your process.

a curiosity, an open door, through which He reaches to spark relationships with other members of His creation. And they're open to His approach because they've been observing your life, the way you live it, and what results from the way you live it.

It's important that your process, the way you do things, leads back to Him. When people retrace your steps, when they look at your conduct, when they see how you do things, it must lead back to Him.

It must provide a proper representation of who He is.

It must show evidence of Him at work in your life.

It must provide an example of what life in relationship with Him is like.

Why?

In college, I was a music minor for 2.5 seconds. For my jazz history class, we had to do a research project. I chose to do mine on Charlie Parker. If you don't know anything about Parker, aka "Bird," he was an incredible jazz musician who basically ushered in the Bebop era, helping jazz become regarded as a bona fide art form. He was known for his improvisational genius, which he played at break neck speeds. Other jazz musicians of the time loved Parker; they practically worshipped him. The thing about Parker is that he was a heroin addict, and his devotees began to attribute his musical genius to the heroin. Wanting to play like him, they began to emulate the process they thought made Parker play like he did. They thought it was the heroin, so they started using heroin.

I find it tragically fascinating how a generation of artists walked into heavy drug use through their observation of someone they admired. When they retraced his steps, in their mind, the steps to genius started with heroin.

When people retrace the steps of your process, where will they end up? What will they be led to?

What will they discover was the source of your accomplishment?

When you allow Him to lead you, the Father can be glorified in your process. It can facilitate a relationship between Him and unreached parts of His creation. It can also contribute the Kingdom perspective to the larger cultural conversation, showing how Kingdom people operate and displaying its more excellent ways.

What does God's way look like in the processes of creating your art and managing your career?

What does it look like to collaborate with Him on composing a song, editing a film, mixing paint colors, choreographing a dance, or negotiating a contract?

> 2 Cor. 6:16 (KJV)
> "And what agreement hath the temple of God with idols? For ye are the temple of the living God; as God hath said, 'I will dwell in them, and walk in them; and I will be their God, and they shall be my people.'"

The Amplified Bible says God will dwell and walk in, with, and among us. This word *dwell* means to "dwell in one and influence him (Gr. *Enoikeo)*." According to Webster's Unabridged, to *walk* is to "move about in visible or otherwise perceptible forms, to pursue a course of action, continue in union."

What God is telling us here is that He moves about His earth in us and through us, making Himself visible in the world through the actions He influences us to take.

The way God structures His statement is interesting. He says, "I will" and "I will be." These are future simple and future continuous statements, implying intention and continuous action.
Does God want to be involved in what we make? Absolutely.
Does He want to be involved in choosing our dancers? Absolutely.
In choosing pieces for our installation?
In writing our grants?
In signing our contracts?
In choosing our agent? Absolutely!
God's intention and desire to collaborate with us as artists is real, even though we don't think He'd want to be involved in the kind of art we make.

So, okay…He wants to be involved.
But in what capacity?
As a dictator? A reviewer? A manager? A collaborator?

As a dictator, He would direct forcefully, imposing His will on us, overriding and punishing any opposition from us. His relationship to us would be distant as He tossed commands at us, expecting us to simply obey.

As a manager, His interaction with us would consist of giving us directives and making sure we completed them. His relationship to us would still be distant, but He wouldn't deal with us as ruthlessly as a dictator.

As a reviewer, He'd have no interaction with us during our process, only with what we produce. His only function would be to approve, or reject, what we do.

But as a collaborator, He would be part of the process from conception, to planning and implementation, sharing His counsel along the way; intending that His contributions influence the decisions and courses of action we end up taking.

How do we collaborate with God this way?

> Ps. 32:8
> "I will instruct you and teach you in the way you should go; I will guide you with My eye."
> *The eyes are used to focus on an object or location. They indicate intention. God will show us what He's focused on, what has His attention, and what He intends for it.*

> Prov. 8:12 (KJV)
> "I wisdom dwell with prudence, and find out knowledge of witty inventions."
> *Need a witty idea? Tap into wisdom!*

> Prov. 2:6
> "For the LORD gives wisdom; From His mouth *come* knowledge and understanding;"
> *The Lord will bring ingenuity into your creative process. He will show you new and fresh ways of putting elements together in your art, setting up your business, pitching your project, marketing your show, funding your company, training your dancers, etc.*

> Prov. 16:3 (AMP)
> "Roll your works upon the Lord [commit and trust them wholly to Him; He will cause your thoughts to become agreeable to His will, and] so shall your plans be established and succeed."
> *Wow! Does anything else need to be said about that?*

> Isa. 30:21
> "Your ears shall hear a word behind you, saying, 'This *is* the way, walk in it,' Whenever you turn to the right hand, Or whenever you turn to the left."
> *In Isaiah's day, they did not have the Spirit of God living on the inside of them so they heard God's voice from outside. As New Covenant Christians, we hear God's voice from within us because we are His temple and He dwells in us.*

1 Jn. 2:27
"But the anointing which you have received from Him abides in you, and you do not need that anyone teach you; but as the same anointing teaches you concerning all things, and is true, and is not a lie, and just as it has taught you, you will abide in Him."
The anointing will be so attentive in tutoring you on how to get the most out of the gifts He's given you.

Prov. 16:9: "A man's heart plans his way, but the Lord directs His steps."

As artists in Christ, we're on a God-journey using gifts He gave us, pursuing a vision He planted in us. Since we're on His journey, using His gifts, pursuing something He initiated in us, it would make sense that He would best know how our gifts could and should be used, what they can do,
how far they can be stretched,
and how to get all the way into what He showed us.

Prov. 3:5-6 says,
"Trust in the Lord with all your heart; and lean not unto your own understanding. In all your ways, acknowledge Him, and He shall direct your paths."

We have the skill and ability to construct our own paths and make our own decisions. We've been given a mind, a will, emotions and the ability to choose. We've been given a personality and inclinations, intelligence and instinct. He's given us intellect, intuition, reason, and the ability to plan, organize, and strategize. We've nurtured a perspective on the world around us.

Being in relationship with God doesn't mean we stop using those faculties. He doesn't expect us to abandon them all for Him. He wants us to engage in them all *with* Him. He wants us to use them under His influence and employ them by His leading. All these tools are ours to complete all the creative impulses He places in our heart. He just wants us to do it with Him.

There's a difference between asking God to bless what we've already set in place, and letting Him lead us in the actual deciding: from what we do, to how we do it, when we do it, and with whom. There's a difference in asking Him to lead us in what we've conjured up, and seeking Him about what we should be doing in the first place. This doesn't mean we can't make plans. It just means we have to be led in forming and executing the plan. Or, it means we have to be flexible enough to receive adjustments, or replacements, to our plan if God has another way.

Now, there are many things that we do in everyday life that He doesn't micro-manage. He's not interested in dictating every nano-second of our day. There are times when He doesn't lead us at all. Instead, He allows us to make the decisions. Just like we're pleased to see our children and students flex their training and find their voice, God is pleased in watching us do the same in His image and likeness. If you've invited Him into your next move, and He allows you to take the lead, then spread your wings and let your imagination run.

Whether He leads us directly, or allows us to exercise our maturity in a situation, there's so much liberty as an artist in relationship with God. There really is. However, that liberty must be anchored by an acknowledgement that we have accountability as a son. 1 Cor. 6:20 says, "You were bought at a price, Therefore glorify God in your bodies." Navigating your art life as a son is understanding you're a steward with great latitude, not an owner with carte blanche. Still, you're only responsible for following the direction He gives you. But, you're also responsible for checking if He has any instructions for what you're about to do, before you do it.

What might His leading actually look like in the processes of your art life?

Creatively, He might tell you to throw a little yellow on a spot when you're painting. He might say take *that line to the right a little more*. In the dance studio, you might do a move and He might say *turn your head to the right when you do that next time. Cross your right leg over the left, then step to the back.*

Business-wise, we go on auditions, we're signing contracts, we're making decisions, we're hiring people, firing people, making choices between locations. The Holy Spirit might say *go talk to the lady in yellow.*
You know what? Don't sign that contract today.
Go stand in the front, on the left, for this audition.
Before you go on that audition, put on that purple shirt that you bought the other day.
Ask that man to explain what it means to option your movie.

Socially, He might tell you to *ask that young lady to lunch.*
Bring your boss flowers.
Write that actor a card and bring it to him tomorrow.
Stop by your agent's office and just ask how they're doing.

I engage with God regularly in the processes of my art life as a teacher, choreographer, and artistic director. I taught modern, tap, and choreography at an arts high school in downtown Los Angeles. I was tremendously blessed with the opportunity to co-create the dance program from scratch. I'm also the Artistic Director/Choreographer for my own dance company, Speak Hill Dance Project. My work is made in the simple appreciation of beautiful bodies moving in space to compelling music. I don't teach at a Christian school and most of the people I interact with are not Christian. What does my collaboration with God in these areas look like?

As a teacher, I seek Him in planning my curriculum and lessons. I pray over the space I'm teaching in before my students arrive. I seek Him about how to get through to a student or how to encourage them. I speak life into my students as He leads me. I pray about corrections to give, ways to explain things clearly, and new combinations and exercises to help my students get better. I pray for the institution and leadership.

As an Artistic Director, I engage with Him over the vision for the company. I pray for, and over my dancers. I speak life into them as He leads me. I ask Him what they're supposed to get from working with me besides dance moves. I ask Him for wisdom for all of the logistical tasks I must handle. I ask Him to send me people, the right people, who will help me bring this vision forward. I pray for favor and open doors, for influence, exposure, and opportunities to present my work to people of influence.

As a choreographer, I pray over a piece before I start. I invite the Holy Spirit into my rehearsals. I ask for His creative help, to expand me as a dance maker, to help me see new ways of moving bodies and assembling movements together. I ask Him for guidance in titling a piece, in finding the music, and in fleshing out a concept through movement. These are just some of the ways I collaborate with God in my creative practice. As I acknowledge Him, thoughts, images, strategies, and courses of action begin to reveal themselves and we enjoy a continuous exchange throughout the process.

What does God's way look like in the processes of creating your art and managing your career?

PRODUCT

The last part of the art life is the product, or the actual artwork. This is where the fight between faith and art usually lives. The big elephant-question at the center of this fight is, *What can (should) Christians make art about?* It's also *What should Christians be making art for?* However, I really hope we're beyond that usefulness-only nonsense.

Okay, so let's talk about it.

Is there anything that Christians can't make art about? If you answer yes, what's your reasoning for why they can't make art about whatever you think they can't make art about? I'm going to address three reasons people might think Christians can't make art about anything and everything.

The first reason is usefulness; and to that I ask the following: Does everything Christians produce, and every interaction we have with people, have to lead to someone getting saved? Is the only plausible end for our art and interaction to evangelize? Did every interaction that Christ had center around the singular goal of getting them saved?

If your answers are yes, I believe you hold a valid conviction; but one that prevents such rich opportunity to display the wonders and joy of life in God in a more meaningful and sophisticated way. It also ignores the reality that there's life after salvation.

The second reason was brought up in one of our KAI Intensive discussions.

In the discussion, I asked if it was ever okay for a Christian to make art about porn. I wasn't asking if it was okay to make a porn film. I was asking if it was okay to make art *about* porn. As you can imagine, I got some interesting looks, particularly after I shared that I thought it was okay. Then I asked them these two questions:

"Has porn disappeared just because you got saved?" They answered no.

"Has your awareness of porn vanished since you've been saved?" They answered no.

I went on to ask, "So even after salvation, Christians still live in a world where porn exists, they're aware that it exists, and they have to manage themselves in its existence. Would you agree?"

They answered yes.

I asked, "Then why can't we make art about that? Why can't we make art about how the Christian encounters porn and manages themselves (or doesn't) in a world where it exists? Why can't we talk about how anyone deals with it? Why can't we talk about its allure? Why can't we talk about the conditions that make it more alluring than it would've been if those conditions were different?"

Then we got into an AMAZING conversation.

In the amazing conversation that ensued, one of the participant's brought up Phil. 4:8.

> "Finally, brethren, whatever things are true, whatever things *are* noble, whatever things *are* just, whatever things *are* pure, whatever things *are* lovely, whatever things *are* of good report, if *there is* any virtue and if *there is* anything praiseworthy—meditate on these things."

Isn't this what we should be focused on as Christians? I would wholeheartedly agree that it's where we should be focused. But for me, that verse doesn't say that we can't address, confront, question, investigate, and deconstruct the things we come up against in our humanity.

I Peter 5:8
"Be sober, be vigilant [alert]; because your adversary the devil walks about like a roaring lion, seeking whom he may devour."

2 Cor. 2:11
"lest Satan should take advantage of us; for we are not ignorant of his devices."

In 2 Cor. 2:10, Paul first tells the Corinthians to make sure they forgive because not doing so is one of the ways the enemy gets in. My point with 1 Ptr. 5:8 and 2 Cor. 2:11 is that we can't be sober, alert, and aware if we aren't even willing to talk about unpleasant things, or acknowledge that they're an issue we face as humans, even though we're now saved. This even impacts our ability to evangelize. How can we be used to free people from things we're not even willing to acknowledge or discuss?

I was talking to a visual artist who was telling me about workshops she taught on the art of confession. In these workshops, she led participants in creating art to, basically, exorcise whatever they were dealing with internally. I thought this was fascinating. For her, it was a personal exercise. However, she explained that some artists use this as their modality for the art they sell. And people buy it. And I can totally understand why they buy it. They look at it and they say, *This person gets me. They understand where I am.* Sometimes, people just need to feel seen before they're ever ready to make any steps towards healing. Sometimes, being understood and validated in their experience *is* the healing.

The third reason I believe people don't think all topics are a go is this question: *How is this topic, this art piece, glorifying God? How is this worship?*

In Romans 12, Paul shows us that our worship (or at least part of it) is to offer ourselves up as vessels that will live for God. In John 17, Jesus gives us insight into what it means to glorify God when He says, "I have glorified You on the earth. I have finished the work which You have given Me to do."

If we're collaborating with the Spirit of God in our creative process,
if we're following His lead,
and this is where He leads us,
and we go where He's leading us,
how is He not being worshipped or glorified in what we talk about?

I guess the bigger question is whether we believe God would lead us to such subject matter in the first place. I leave that between you and God in your individual walk with Him. I know He does for many artists; and to them I want to say *Go on and do what the Lord is putting on your heart. Stop worrying about what it looks like.*

I believe the key and encompassing issue to this whole thing is worldview. The larger mandate for us, as believers, is to live, converse, and engage from a Kingdom worldview. That provides a much larger palette for artists than the narrow vocabulary and subject matter used in Christian circles, among Christians talking to other Christians for "Christian" purposes.

If we focus on worldview, it becomes less about the topics in our art, and more about the lens and perspective we take *on* the topic.

> Ecclesiastes 3:1-8 (KJV)
> "To every [thing there is] a season, and a time to every purpose under the heaven: A time to be born, and a time to die; a time to plant, and a time to pluck up [that which is] planted; A time to kill, and a time to heal; a time to break down, and a time to build up; A time to weep, and a time to laugh; a time to mourn, and a time to dance; A time to cast away stones, and a time to gather stones together; a time to embrace, and a time to refrain from embracing; A time to get, and a time to lose; a time to keep, and a time to cast away; A time to rend, and a time to sew; a time to keep silence, and a time to speak; A time to love, and a time to hate; a time of war, and a time of peace."

The word "time" in this passage is the Hebrew word, *eth,* and it includes experiences, events, occurrences, and occasions. If it's acceptable to laugh, then it must also be acceptable to engage in things that make us laugh. If all we ever explore in our art is the death, burial, and resurrection of Christ, where's the stimulus and occasion to engage in raucous laughter?

Following this line of thinking, these "times," expressed in Ecclesiastes, open up the whole of the human experience for us to explore. The key is exploring them from a mindset illuminated by our relationship with God and His word. We aren't obligated to force all our artistic content into an evangelistic frame. We're only obligated to share, question, and celebrate life in a way that embodies the Kingdom's influence and impact on our life;
to manifest how it's worldview underpins everything we produce,
frames our perspective,
influences our character and conduct,
and permeates our daily practice and artistic process.

4 The How of In, but not Of

We are talking about being unapologetic in our "secular" art career. Immediately, we're performing a root transfer, uprooting the mess of our supposed "offenses" and replacing them with the truth of being an artist in Christ. We just finished addressing the perception that our kind of art careers don't fulfill our Christian responsibility to worship God, honor and glorify Him, or build the kingdom.

The three remaining "offenses" are:

- Such an art life compromises the Christian, who will inevitably fall into darkness by association.

- Such an art life taints God's pure and holy creation, by mixing it in that world, with those people.

- Such an art life betrays God's goodness to us by taking His gifts and using them for anything other than relationship and service.

I believe we've sufficiently tackled this last one in our usefulness conversation.

In this next section, I want to tackle those first two "offenses" together, as they both deal with the issue of association. Basically, people are concerned with two things:
1. How do we exist within the culture of our "secular" art career without taking on the culture which governs and defines it?
2. How do we interact with the people within that culture, who live under a different paradigm than our own?

These two concerns highlight a simple reality: we're dealing with two different cultures (mindsets, customs, practices, and values) and have to understand how they interact. When we don't know how to interact, we fall prey to fears and insecurities about our effectiveness, our motives, our identity, and our allegiance.

I want to tackle this issue of association in two parts:
1. The issue of existing in another culture.
2. The issue of taking on a different culture.

Existing in another culture

Since 2016, I spend time in Europe once a year. I was really pushing to have this book finished before I left for Europe in the summer of 2017. I got all but the last section done, which at the time was about this very issue. I was really irritated that I didn't meet my deadline; but as my time in Europe went on, I began to see God's wisdom in the delay.

One night, I had finally gotten my head together to continue writing and the Lord took me down a train of thought. I started thinking about my presence as a U.S. citizen in Spain. There was an established culture that existed here before I arrived. And I belong to an established culture that I left to come here, and still represent even though I'm here. How do these two cultures interact?

What is my place here as a foreigner?

What is my responsibility to this established culture that I'm entering?

What is my responsibility to the culture I come from?

Where do they cross?

Where do they merge?

And where do they simply live beside one another?

How do these play out in the reasons I came into this other culture in the first place?

These are the same questions we must consider as Christians taking space in "secular" culture.

So, what is my place as a U.S. citizen in Spain?

Is it to make Spain more "American?"
Is it to abandon my Americanism and embrace the Spanish ethos?
Is it to try to avoid Spanish culture completely and set up a little
"American" enclave within Spain for myself?
Is it to appreciate, and participate in, Spanish culture in ways that
nourish my own?
Well, that would depend on my purpose for being here. Likewise, our
place as Christians in "secular" culture depends on our purpose for
being there.

There are four ways we typically interact with "secular" culture: either as
flounders, hermits, imperialists, or ambassadors.

Flounders

Flounders are interesting fish. They're flat and are known for changing
their color to blend into the ocean floor. They use this ability for one
purpose: to survive. They survive by taking on the attributes of their
environment. By Romans 12:2, we know this is not our purpose as
Christians in "secular" culture. We're not to take on the world's ways,
and we're there for much more than to just survive.

What puts us in survival mode as artists in Christ out there?
I believe it's fear.
We're afraid that people are out to get us in a post-Christian (but really
past-Christian) culture.

We're afraid that people won't accept us for who we are, that they won't
see past us being a Christian. And if they can't see past us being a
Christian, they'll miss out on our artistic contribution. Or worse, we'll
never be allowed to make a contribution in the first place.

We're afraid that we won't get access if we're not doing what everyone
else is doing. As artists, we exist in a strange paradox. We want to stand
out, but we want to be noticed in a way that distinguishes, not isolates,
us.

We're afraid we'll lose friends and opportunities if we're found out, that we'll be pigeonholed and lumped in with "those" Christians. We don't want to be seen in that light.

We're afraid that our Christian identity will overshadow and hinder our artistic identity. We have somewhere to go to be out and proud as Christians. But we can't really be the same as artists there. Our art careers are our place to be out and proud as artists and we don't want anything to mess that up. We don't want our faith to impede our artistic journey. We don't want our Christianity to reduce our artistic impact.

We're afraid of falling prey to judgment and exclusion, of being mischaracterized.

We're afraid of being seen as simple.

We're afraid of being inadequate at standing up for our faith in a sophisticated way.

Hermits

Hermits withdraw themselves from the surrounding population. They live in isolation. Some of us have hermit tendencies, where we isolate ourselves from interacting with the culture, making little enclaves among our own. We only associate with Christians. We only work with other Christians.

What leads us to this withdrawing, sticking-to-our-own tendency?
Some of us believe it's the holy thing to do, that it's what God wants.
Some of it is choice; it's just easier to deal with.
But some of it is fear.
We don't want to compromise our faith.
We don't want to dilute our conviction.
We don't want to be perceived as compromising or shifting in our allegiance.

Imperialists

There are a great number of Christians who believe our duty is to be imperialists, to take over "secular" culture. But tell me this: where do we see God ever commission His people as cultural imperialists? Where in the Bible do we ever see the precedent for taking over another culture? Where does He ever tell His people to impose Godly rule on a pagan nation?

Did Daniel work to impose the Law on the Chaldeans?

Did Joseph on the Egyptians?

Did God tell the apostles and the church to overthrow the Roman government, to obliterate the Gentile and Samaritan way of life? Did He even tell them to expel the sorcerers?

No, He didn't; because we're not in culture to be imperialists. We're ambassadors of the kingdom of the most high God (2 Cor. 5:20).

Since we're ambassadors, we better find out more about them.

Ambassadors

What is an ambassador?

What makes them effective at what they do?

And what does this tell us about being artists in Christ interacting in "secular" culture?

An ambassador represents their home government within a foreign government. While there, they build relationships and engage in acts of diplomacy in order to represent and further their home government's interests.

What makes them effective?

First, ambassadors understand they are guests within the foreign government. They conduct their activity in a way that respects the governance of the sovereign hosting them. Ambassadors are given access that affords them the opportunity to advance their home nation's interests. They're given this opportunity because they compose themselves with the consideration that they're a guest in someone else's space.

The second thing that makes them effective is that they know the secret to their effectiveness. Remember, the whole reason they're in a foreign government is to advance their home government's interests. But they know the best way to accomplish this is relationship. Remember when we talked about the undercover officer, who uses relationship to get access to criminal activity? They don't get access by just being present. They gain it by finding common ground. Then they gain proximity, and eventually permission, by adding value through serving.

The third thing that makes them effective is that they understand they're in a long-game operation. Diplomacy takes finesse and patience. It takes wisdom to advance one's interests in a foreign environment without offending their sensibilities or arousing hostility. It also takes time to assess the relationship to discover ways to act that benefits both parties. Inter-governmental relationships fare better when there is mutual benefit.

The fourth thing that makes ambassadors effective is their confidence. They know their government supports them. They know it has their back. They know they have the authority to be present in the foreign government and interact with its nation on their own government's behalf. This liberates them to do what they need to do.

Now, what does this tell us about being Christians existing as ambassadors in "secular" society?

Before we delve into that, let's connect back into the larger conversation we're having. We're in the process of uprooting misinformation, and planting roots of truth about being an artist in Christ working in "secular" culture. We're doing this by addressing four "offenses" our art careers are perceived to be committing. The two we're currently tackling deal with the issue of association. Association brings the concern of existing within a different culture and interacting with its citizens without taking on its ways or their behaviors.

We started this discussion by looking at our role within that culture, which we said was as ambassadors. Now, we're about to see what we can glean from what they do and how they work.

Many of us experience trepidation when we think about associating with non-Christians on any deep and meaningful level.

What is that about?

I think we have to address this from under the cloud of evangelism.
Why evangelism?
Because when we think about non-Christians, we have a tendency to reduce our interactions with them to getting them saved.
So, evangelism…
Some of us are over-zealous about it.
The thought of having to pursue people to talk about Jesus freaks others of us out.
Some of us have been led to believe getting them saved is the only reason we'd ever associate with a non-Christian.
Some of us question this, finding it very natural to engage with non-Christians, which leads to a whole other set of issues:
Am I doing enough as a Christian?
What should I be doing?
What will other Christians think about me?
Am I compromising my faith?
Am I losing my faith if I find similarities and common ground with non-Christians?
And on and on.

Hopefully, what we're about to jump into will help alleviate a lot of that anxiety.

As the people of God, we're representing His interest in a foreign government.

What is His interest?

It's reconciliation: the restoration of the relationship between God and His creation (people, planet, and systems operating on the planet). Our art careers are how we take space and engage within this foreign government; but facilitating reconciliation is the reason we're there taking space in the first place. This is our ambassadorship.

What makes us effective?

First, we said that ambassadors understand, and respect, the reality that they're guests. Now, this is a very interesting, and to some, almost heretical, notion: us being guests when our God owns the planet and all of creation (Ps. 24:1).

How does that work?

Well, it's true that it all belongs to Him. We all belong to Him (Ps. 50:12 / Job 41:11). So, then where does this foreign government come into play? And why do we even have to consider it if everything belongs to God? Let's answer that with an analogy.

I own a duplex: one building with two apartments. I live in one apartment and I've rented out the other. I own the whole building, and I have ultimate authority over it. However, I only have immediate authority over the apartment in which I live. When I rented out the second apartment, the renter signed a lease where we both agreed they would have immediate authority over that one. Even though I own the whole building, and have ultimate authority over it, I must respect the immediate authority my renter has over the second apartment for the term of their lease. As long as it doesn't violate the terms of the lease, I have to respect however that renter wants to live within that apartment. This means I can't just walk into their apartment whenever I want.

I can't just go in and claim their stuff as my own just because I own the building.
I can't dictate their living style just because it's different than mine.

For the term of their lease, that's their space. I have to treat it as their space. I have to conduct myself as if I'm in someone else's space, even though I own the building. If I'm ever permitted to go into their space, I must respect their governance of that space.

How does this apply to our conversation?

For a period of time, another governance is being allowed to exist on God's earth. Technically, everything belongs to Him. But the garden mishap activated a leasing arrangement that brought in another governing tenant. So, on God's earth, we have His system of governance and the enemy's system of governance.

The earth is God's building.
The kingdom of God is the first apartment.
The world's system ("secular" culture) is the second apartment.
And, for a period of time, there's a leasing agreement in effect where the enemy is able to govern this second apartment space however he wishes. In that space, for this period of time, his system is the norm. It's the grain, the current, the matrix. It's the default way of being.

In Luke 4:6, Satan tells Jesus that the authority and glory of the earth's kingdoms are his. He lies about them being delivered to him; he stole them through deception. But through the deception, he did, in fact, assume authority over the kingdoms of this world. In 2 Cor. 4:4, he's called the god of this age. In John 12:31, 14:30, and 16:11, Jesus refers to him as the ruler of this world. So, there's a way this world is being ruled. And there's God's way.

As Christians in "secular" culture, it's like us going into that second apartment. We're in another tenant's space. In that norm, we, the people of God, are foreigners and guests (1 Ptr. 2:11). That is not our system.

Well, now, hold on, Marlita. Are you saying that we're supposed to just let the enemy roam and reign freely?

No, not at all.

When I was writing this whole guest bit, I imagined lips pursing and eyes shifting at that word: Guest.
I get it.
I understand how spiritually counterintuitive that sounds, especially when our Dad owns it all.

Mt. 11:12 tells us that the "kingdom of God suffers violence, and the violent take it by force."
David, a man of God, looked at Goliath and scoffed, "Who is this uncircumcised Philistine that he should defy the armies of the living God?"
Rev. 11:15 tells us that the kingdoms of this world are to be made the kingdoms of our Lord.

And I'm not arguing against any of these, or trying to minimize our responsibility to take them up.

Instead, I'm speaking to *how* we accomplish them.

You see, an ambassador must employ diplomacy when advancing their nation's interests. They must further them without offense or arousing hostility. Now, let me clarify that because Jesus clearly tells us that we'll be hated because we're His. So, how do these two coexist? The message will offend and arouse hostility because it pins people in a corner and demands a decision. But, we are not to offend in our manner, in how we interact with people. They may not like what we have to say, but they shouldn't be able to complain about the way we are when we say it (Col. 4:6).

Any strategies or tactics ambassadors use have to be employed in a way that doesn't destroy their chances of fulfilling the whole purpose of them being there in the first place.

Yes, the violent take it by force; but that force is to be directed toward the enemy, as we don't wrestle against flesh and blood. We're to direct spiritual violence toward the enemy on behalf of the person.
We fight for them.
We don't fight them.
As guests, our violence and boldness has to be used with great care, and employed with strategic precision. We have to be careful not to make people casualties of war when reconciling them is the whole point of the war. We have to wage war with wisdom, a strategic wisdom.

What does that look like?

When we go into "secular" culture, it's doing so respecting the reality that there's a leasing agreement in effect, and that people have free will to choose which apartment they want to live in.

Here's the deal:

We're born into sin (Rom. 5:12-19). This sin I'm talking about is not acts that we willingly commit, but rather a state of being. It's more like saying I was born in the state of California. That has nothing to do with anything I did. It just speaks to the geographical location I was born into. Said another way, all of us are born into that second apartment space, and into the culture that shapes everything happening in that space.
To move from that state, that culture, that second apartment, one must choose to do so, and act on that choice. They have to willingly choose to live outside the norm, go against the grain, swim against the current, unplug from the matrix.

The important thing to note here is that they can choose whichever space they want to be in. We were given the same choice. We've made our choice to unplug from the matrix we were born into. We chose to move out of that second apartment and into the first one. Still, we can't ever forget that we were given a choice. And we have to give others the same room.

In Mk. 8:34 and Rev. 22:17 (KJV), the Lord uses the phrase "whosoever will." This means that room has been given for whosoever will not. And, we have to respect the right of those who will not, to not, just as God respects it. So, if we're going to go into that second apartment space, we can't expect them to live, there, by the rules of the first apartment. We're not in the first apartment.
We're in the second apartment, which already has an established culture. And in that space, we are guests.

This is why it's important to understand that we're ambassadors, not imperialists. Ambassadors gain the opportunity to advance their nation's interests because they respect what it means to be a guest in someone else's space. Instead, they focus on making themselves a good guest.

What makes a good guest?

What makes us a guest that keeps getting invited to more events?
Into events in more exclusive and intimate circles?
What gets us invited to the dinner with the friends you have to pass several tests to meet?
How do we become a guest that our host feels all their friends *need* to meet?
This privilege is given when we add value to the occasion and the people in it. What we carry is fragrant. It's luminous, preserving, and life-giving. It adds to our environment and relationships when we know how to yield it.

This leads to the second key to our effectiveness, which is knowing the secret of our effectiveness: relationship.

5 The Power of Good

Now, as I mentioned before, quite a few of us struggle with having relationships with non-Christians on any deep and meaningful level. Either we hesitate in doing it, or wonder if something might be wrong with us because it happens so effortlessly. Then, there are those who understand nothing is wrong with it; who understand it's what we're supposed to be doing.

Again, as Christians, we have a high tendency to see these relationships through the tainted goggles of evangelism. Am I saying we're not supposed to care about evangelism? No. But I am pointing out that we've mastered the most ineffective ways of doing it.

I think it all boils down to a simple fear of being overtaken, in the various ways that applies. Let's address that.

First, we don't have to be afraid of being overtaken in relationship with non-Christians.
Why?
1 Jn. 4:4 and 5:4 tell us that God, in us, is greater than he that's in the world, and that we've overcome anything in the world through Christ.

Second, we don't have to be afraid because it's not our association that compromises us. It's not something bad rubbing off on us that corrupts us. In Mk. 7:18-23, Jesus explains that it's what's within a person that corrupts them, not anything that touches them from outside. So, if your heart is right before God, if your trust is in Him, and you're being led by

Him, there's nothing that you encounter with non-Christians that will cause you to falter or change course.

Ok, with that out of the way, let's look at this relationship deal.

Prov. 11:30 tells us he who wins souls is wise. The wisdom regarding people is that you gain access through common ground, and permission through adding value. John C. Maxwell speaks to this with his 101% principle, where you basically find the 1% you have in common, and focus 99% of your energy on that 1%. This, again, is the undercover officer, who uses relationship to get access to criminal activity. They don't get access by just being present. They gain it by, first, finding common ground. Then they gain proximity, and eventually permission, by adding value through serving and contributing.

As artists, finding common ground with non-Christians in our career life should be easy.
We're both creative.
We both respect good art.
We're both in the career grind.
We respect artistic process.
We both find inspiration from the same director.
And on and on.

That seems easy enough, right?
Just be a creative vibing about the world of creativity with another creative.
But, how do we add value to them?
Isn't a relationship with God the highest value we can add to someone's life?
No, not when they don't perceive that as valuable.

What do I mean?

People generally only allow us into one dimension of intimacy at a time. When we serve them, or contribute to their life, we have to do so at their pace, at what's appropriate for the level of access they've granted us. Looking through the eyes of Spanish culture, speaking about faith into one's life is a very intimate act. We have to wait until we have clearance for that level of intimacy. It might take a long time before they ever see a relationship with God as something that would add value to their own life. They need time to observe the value it adds to yours before they can consider the possibility of it in their own.

So, we have to look at how we add value to their life outside of the getting-them-saved conversation. If you don't know how to do this, you'll never get to the salvation conversation in any way they'll receive.

Ok, how do we do it?

Well, the obvious way is to just be a good friend. Be a person who can be trusted, who encourages them and speaks life to them. If you genuinely get to know someone (and not just get to know them enough to get them saved and move on), considerate ways to enrich their life will become obvious.

Another way we serve them is by fighting on their behalf. Remember that whole bit where we talked about the violent taking things by force? Well, this is where we unleash that force and violence behind the scene through intercession.

We do this by praying against spiritual blindness (2 Cor. 4:4 / Acts 26:18).

We do it by praying that they see the goodness of God at work in your life and in theirs.

We do it by praying that all the barriers keeping them from responding to Him be removed.

We do it by praying for courage to fill their heart so they can take the leap and unplug from the matrix.

We can do this behind the scenes while keeping our in-person conversation to our mutual love of Tarentino films, 8mm shooting, Jiri Kylian's choreography, etc – that is, until (or if ever) they give us permission to speak to more intimate things like salvation.

A third way we add value in the relationship is by being who we are (as those carrying the presence of God) on their behalf. The Bible says we are salt, light, fragrance, and love. When we embrace these attributes, and dispense them freely, we add value to their life by God's grace. Let's look at how.

Salt of the Earth

Salt is an interesting element. It's necessary for life to thrive and its usefulness extends into all parts of human technology, from water processing to agriculture and highway preparation.

Preservative

Salt is a preservative that prevents decay, infection, and spoilage. It also keeps things safe from injury, harm, and destruction.

When revealing his identity to his brothers, who had sold him into slavery, Joseph informs them that God sent him before them to preserve them in Egypt's great famine, and to save their lives by a great deliverance. He assures them that he'll take care of them and keep them safe from poverty (Gen. 45:7-11).

God was willing to honor Abraham and preserve the entire wicked city of Gomorrah for the sake of ten righteous people, if Abraham could find them (Gen. 8:32).

How do we serve our relationships as preservers?
Through praying and interceding for our career community, we usher in the preserving power of the Spirit of God as we stand in the gap for the individuals in it. In Ps. 106:23 and Ezek. 22:30, we see a focus on individuals interceding for others to keep them from destruction. We not only intercede for them to be preserved from ultimate destruction through salvation, but also from the more immediate threats of the enemy against their life (1 Ptr. 5:8).

Guard

Salt can be used to prevent things from being able to grow or produce. It was an ancient custom to sow a defeated city with salt so that nothing could grow there. Abimelech did this in Jdgs. 9:45 when he seized the city of Shechem.

In our environments, in the lives of our career community, we can declare things illegal that do not line up with the word of God. Mt. 18:18 tells us "whatever we bind [declare illegal] on earth will be bound [declared illegal] in heaven, and whatever we loose [declare legal] on earth will be loosed [declared legal] in heaven." Through our prayer, intercession, and declaration, we have the authority to put our foot down, salt the earth and declare "not in this gallery, not in these dancers, not in this negotiation, not in this collaboration." If it doesn't line up with Kingdom protocol, God has given you and I authority to release our salt and stop it from remaining and producing.

Fertilizer

Salt can promote growth when used as a fertilizer. It increases the productivity of the soil by supplying nutrients or making existing nutrients available.

Prov. 10:11 says "the mouth of a righteous man is a well of life."
The words we speak stimulate life in people, situations, and environments.

Prov. 10:21 says "the lips of the righteous nourish many."
By the words we speak to the situations and people around us, we act as a fertilizer helping to stimulate and bring forth the productive things in them. Our words, under the inspiration of the Holy Spirit, stimulate life by releasing the spiritual nutrients they need to thrive.

Booster

Salt enhances the flavor already present in the food to which it's added.

Rom. 11:29 (KJV) tells us the "gifts and calling of God are without repentance." The NKJV says they're irrevocable. Whether a person ever acknowledges and accepts Christ as their Lord, the gifts God put in them still remain. When we build relationship with people, we stimulate those gifts, connecting them closer to their identity and purpose. We stimulate the awareness of something bigger than themselves, even if we never see them get saved.

Jn. 1:9 tells us that God lights every person who comes into the world. That's every person, not just every Christian person. Every one of us are born with a sense of dual citizenship, feeling like we have a connection to something beyond this physical world. We all battle this nagging sense that there's another part of ourselves we have to connect with to be fully whole. It's as if we all came into this world holding a key with a note on it saying, "Come home." We spend our whole lives putting this key into random doors like money, sex, work, and relationships, hoping to find the door it opens. Through relationship, we help enhance the light that has been dimmed inside them, helping them to see that Christ is the door (2 Cor. 4:4).

Change Agent

Salt changes its environment. But it's interesting how it does this. It's stealth. When used prudently, it's unobtrusive. It makes its impact, then it's gone. It dissipates after fulfilling its purpose. You can't see the salt that's added to food, but you can taste it. And you can tell when it's not there. When it's absent, you notice.

Salt interacts with the thing it wants to change. It goes into food and changes it from within. Your presence impacts the lives and environments you encounter. There's supposed to be evidence in you, fruit produced by you, and changes in environments and situations in response to you that make having you around better for everyone. People in your career community may never recognize you're a Christian. They may not recognize that the source of your impact is Christ in you. Some will just say things like *I don't know what it is about you, but things are just better when you're around.*

Light of the World

Mt. 5:14 says that we are the light of the world. We usually misinterpret this, trying to shine light *on* people instead of *for* them. This is probably a big reason many people have issues with Christians. I mean, who wants a light shined in their face?

When I was studying for this section, two kinds of light came to me: the light from a candle and the light from a flashlight. What's the difference between them?

The light from a flashlight is sharp, intense, and piercing. Interaction with it is harsh. Its coverage is narrow, but long, allowing one to see what it's aimed at, but not much more. As Christians, our crusade against the sins of the worldly can be so narrowly focused that we forget we're dealing with human beings with complex reasons for being in the state that we find them (as we were when God found us).

When we shine a flashlight into a person's face, we can see, but they cannot. Though we're using light, we haven't shown them anything, except that we're rude and inconsiderate, and that we don't care about the possible harm we could cause them. This *light at* approach, where we expose people's sins to them, has caused so much damage to so many people's hearts. It's left them despising God and anything having to do with Him.

I get it.

What kind of God would institute the kind of religion that would produce this kind of people? It's interesting, that people take stances on God based on how they're treated by His followers. And it's completely understandable. I mean, think about it: how many times have we seen a child act up and formed an opinion about their parents because of how the child was acting? Or formed an opinion about an entire company based on an encounter with a single employee?
Something to think about.

1 Ptr. 2:12 talks about people observing our good works, glorifying God because of what they observed. But how can they see our good works if we're using our light in a way that blocks their ability to see anything at all?

In contrast to the flashlight, the light from a candle is circular. Its coverage is wide. It doesn't have an aim, it simply serves a purpose. This wider coverage allows one to see more things in the room outside of the object of their focus. It's soft, soothing, and inviting. It's comforting and gives off warmth.

Using our light like a candle provides enough coverage for us to see another person, and for that person to see us. In them, we see more than just their sin, what they do. We see who they are, who God made them. We see those things that are latent, hidden, and forgotten in them. We see the root of the choices they made. And in that, we understand that if they'd known of a better way, or felt like they had a choice, they would've taken it. As light, it's not just our purpose to show them what we're doing, but to also bring attention to what they could be doing as a result of who they, too, could be.

In us, they see what we do. They see how we treat them, how we respond to them and situations, and they make their decisions about us based on those observations. They also make decisions about God based on them. It's showing them our good works, not their filthy, wicked ways that moves them to regard God as good. Remember how I said that people have to observe and experience God at work in your life before they see any value of having Him in their own? This is what I'm talking about.

Now, what are these good works that cause men to regard God positively?

The good works that change a heart are not us refraining from sex, drinking, clubbing, or cursing. Those are good things to do, but they're not changing the hearts of people toward God.
What then?

We find them in Gal. 5:22-23. The good works that cause change come out of the fruit of the Spirit. It's action and interaction that comes from being led and influenced by the Spirit of God. Rom. 2:4 tells us it's the goodness of God that leads one to repentance. People first experience God's goodness through His children being led by Him in dispensing it.

If you pay attention throughout Scripture, you'll find that most of the instruction given is either about how we regard and treat God or how we regard and treat each other. Mt. 22:40 says upon these two things (loving God with all our heart, soul, and mind, and loving our neighbor as ourselves) "hang all the law and the prophets." Basically, every instruction given, and every word spoken by the prophets, is summarized by these two precepts.

The truth revealed.
Another function of light is that it reveals the features of whatever it hits. 2 Cor. 4:4 tells us that people are blinded, unable to see the light of the gospel. When one is blinded, they exist in darkness, unable to see the things around them. They're also unable to see the impact their environment is having on them. As our light shines in the world, it collides with darkness, revealing its futility, its cost, its deception, etc. We do this by our example, until our example opens the door for God's word.

The Fragrance of Christ

2 Cor. 2:14 says that we are the fragrance of Christ.

It says we're the fragrance, not the odor.

Yet, in many of our dealings with people we are odorous in the name of the Lord, not fragrant.

Both are smells that affect the senses, and both cause a reaction in the one who smells them. An odor is an unpleasant smell. It's a smell that repels you, that makes you do things to try to escape it. It agitates you, and makes you crave relief from it.

A fragrance, on the other hand, is a pleasant aroma. When the senses notice it, they want to get closer to it. They seek it out. They want to smell it again and again. When we smell a fragrance that we like, we want to have it around us all the time so that we can smell it all the time. More than that, we want to put it on us so that we can smell like it all the time to other people.

A fragrance arouses interest. It attracts attention and makes people want to engage with the source of the scent. It makes them take an action to inquire about what they smell. It makes them search out what they have to do, and where they have to go, to be able to smell the same way. It interrupts the trajectory of a person. It breaks their concentration on whatever they were focused on, and shifts that focus to the pursuit of the scent.

Think about it: how many times have you walked past a person, smelled their perfume or cologne, and then pursued them to ask what they were wearing? Or how many times have you passed a person with food, smelled it, and then pursued them to find out where they got it?

What would possibly cause that kind of reaction in your career community? What would make them stop what they're doing and take notice of what you're doing, to the point that they would go as far as asking you about it? Let's look.

2 Cor. 2:14 (KJV):
> "Now thanks be unto God, which always causes us to triumph in Christ, and maketh manifest the savour [NKJV says "through us diffuses the fragrance"] of His knowledge by us in every place."

I was taught that you can unearth a lot of richness in a scripture by looking up the words, plugging the definitions into the scripture, and then re-reading the scripture with the definitions included. Below are the definitions of four key words in 2 Cor. 2:14.

- triumph *(Gr. thriameuo)*, to grant complete success.[1]

- manifest *(Gr. phaneroo)*, to become known, to be plainly recognized or thoroughly understood, disclose who and what one is.[2]

- and *(Gr. kai)*, This one is really interesting. It serves a functional purpose in this passage.
1. It designates cause. It marks something [that will inevitably follow] what has been previously said.
2. It makes a declaration that if the first thing happens, the second will be done also.[3]

- place *(Gr. topos)*, speaks to location but also includes occasion, opportunity, and condition.[4]

Now, let's plug those definitions into the verse and see what we find out:

---

[1] Blueletterbible.org
[2] Blueletterbible.org
[3] Webster's Unabridged Dictionary
[4] Webster's Unabridged Dictionary

Now thanks be unto God, which always causes us to [have complete success] in Christ, [which inevitably makes who God is plainly known and recognized and arouses interest in who He is] through our complete success in everything we do.

What is the fragrance of who He is?
What about God pulls the attention of others?
What makes who He is attractive to the non-believer?
What is it that we carry that shows them the kind of God He is *and* causes them to want to know more about Him?

According to 2 Cor. 2:14, it's our complete success in everything we put our hands to do. This doesn't mean that if we experience adversity, we're not releasing the fragrance of Christ. Success is also a state of mind and manner of being. When we have a victorious outlook and a peaceful disposition, even in adversity, that communicates success as well. Let's look at some scripture:

> Deut. 30:9
> "The Lord will make you abound in all the work of your hand, in the fruit of your body, in the increase of your livestock, and in the produce of your land for good. For the Lord will again rejoice over you for good as He rejoiced over your fathers."

> Deut. 28:8
> "The Lord will again command the blessing on you in your storehouses and in all to which you set your hand, and He will bless you in the land which the Lord your God is giving you."

> Deut. 28:12
> "The Lord will open to you His good treasure, the heavens, to give rain to your land in its season, and to bless all the work of your hand."

> Ps. 1:3
> "He (the righteous) shall be like a tree planted by the rivers of water, that brings forth its fruit in its season,

whose leaf also shall not wither; and whatever he does
shall prosper."

I mean, come on! Who wouldn't want to know a God who treats His
children like that? And these are not even a speck of all God's
expressions of His intended goodness to us.

The fragrance of God, what makes Him attractive, is not that He
condemns the sinner, but that He so lavishly loves on His children,
engages Himself in their lives, and invests His whole being in their
success, happiness, and wholeness.

When you're booking jobs,
when your show is receiving rave reviews,
when you make hit, after hit, after hit,
when you receive unwavering loyalty from friends and colleagues,
when you remain at peace and full of joy through adversity,
when people always want to go the extra mile for you,
when your company is operating in the black in a devastating climate,
when God is fulfilling His promises to be good to you,
people will want to know your secret.

Through looking at your success, they'll get a look into who God is and
who He is to His people, and they'll want to know that God. This is
what they'll notice because this is what they're drawn to (Mt. 6:32 / Lk.
12:30). This is what they're pursuing.

Now, some will read this and say *it doesn't take all that. It's not about the
money. I don't do it for the fame. I do it for God and the art.* That's fine and
well, but would you take a seminar on how to become an international
CEO from a homeless man who's on the corner asking you for money?

As Christians, we fail to realize that our holy and righteous living is of
no consequence to the unbeliever. They don't care that we pray, they
criticize us for tithing, and they think we're ridiculously archaic for

abstaining until marriage. They don't have the Spirit of God interacting with them, so they have no regard for the things of God.

Truth be told, because of how they've seen us live, many of them think serving God means they can't live life fully, can't want to be successful, and can't be prosperous. Why would they want to serve someone they believe will take all that stuff away from them?

What makes them stop and pay attention is success, excellence, and prosperity because that's where their focus is. They're in pursuit of the dream of life, liberty, and happiness. And they're pursuing it the only way they know how. Introducing them to a God who's poised to give them that *and* wholeness is a strategic measure by God Himself. He accomplishes it by showing Himself off through our success and excellence in our art, business dealings, and overall endeavors.

In 1 Cor. 9:22, Paul says he becomes all things to all men for the sake of the gospel. We even have to be willing to embrace success, prosperity, and notoriety for the sake of those who will be drawn to the gospel because of it.

Exhibitors and Dispensers of the Love of God

When it comes to interacting with non-Christians, love can be difficult to wrap our head around.

How far does it go?

What does it look like?

How do we do it without compromising God's standard?

This is all the more confusing in this political and cultural climate where any difference of opinion gets you labeled a bigot, racist, fundamentalist, and every other horrible name you can think of. It's difficult to say I care about you but I don't agree with your thinking.

So, what does love look like with people whose lives and philosophies don't line up with the standards and mindset you've built your life around?

I like what 1 Cor. 13:7 (AMPC) says:

"Love bears up under anything *and* everything that comes, is ever ready to believe the best of every person, its hopes are fadeless under all circumstances, and it endures everything [without weakening]."

What does this look like when it comes to our interaction with another person? I like what my pastor taught us. He explained that love toward another person is a decision of who we'll be to them, and how we'll treat them. It's saying *This is the person I'm determining to be in your life. I'll be the same person to you, no matter what you do or say to me. My decision to treat you this way goes beyond you, and will stay the same no matter what I experience or receive from you.*

Okay, that sounds great, in theory. But, what do I do when I'm seeing all kinds of things I don't agree with in my relationships with non-Christians. Doesn't real love tell the truth? Aren't I endorsing their behavior, and worse, sleeping on my job if I don't say something?

Well, let's revisit 1 Cor. 13:7, but this time let's look at the NKJV version. It says love "bears all things, believes all things, hopes all things, endures all things." Here's what it doesn't say, though. It doesn't say that love:
agrees with all things,
allows all things,
excuses all things,
endorses all things, or
participates in all things.

Love does have a standard. It has parameters. I want to share a little formula the Lord gave to me to help me in this balance.
1. Love the person
2. Respect the choice
3. Hold the standard

Love the Person

As Christians, our job in loving other people is to see them as someone for whom Christ also died. It's to see them as someone God also desires to be saved by His love, no matter what we see them doing, and no matter how long we see them doing it. It's to focus on seeing them through His hope for them, and to constantly extend that hope to them. It's regarding them as God does. If they should ever decide they want Him, no matter what they've done or how long they've been doing it, He'll be right there to deliver them and shed His love abundantly on them, just like He did with us.

When God considers us who've accepted His salvation, there's nothing we can do to change His determination to be good to us.
Why?
When He looks at us, He sees Christ in us, not sin in us. He doesn't treat us like we just sinned. He treats us like the person we've been made through the finished work of Christ, even if we don't act like it yet. That's how we have to see them. Not like they've just sinned, but as the person Christ died for them to become.

In doing this, we're not looking at what they're doing and saying it's okay. Truth be told, it's not our place to say anything about what they're doing unless the Holy Spirit directs and releases us to share His hope for them, with them.

In the meantime,
we continue to stand in the gap for them through intercession,
maximize the 1% we agree on,
continue speaking life to them and encouraging what's good in them,
being a Godly example,
and just being a good friend.

Respect the choice

You're in relationship with God.
That's something that you entered into voluntarily.
You made a choice to live your life for God.
The non-Christians around you have not made that same voluntary choice.
They have not agreed to live their life for God like you have.
And that's their right.
They have a right, given to them by God Himself, to live their life however they choose to live it.
Now, there will come a time where every one of us will have to account for how we've lived our life; but, for the time being, we each have a choice in how we live it.

So, you made the choice to live your life for God, and they did not.
And in you choosing to live your life for God, you also agreed to live, and not live, in a certain way.
But it's unfair for you to hold other people, who did not choose what you chose, to those same standards and expectations.
It's unfair to expect them to fall in line with something they neither agreed to, or signed up for.

Further, it's not your responsibility to be the conduct police, or let people know when their behavior is not honoring God.
They never agreed to honor God in the first place.
You did.

So, your responsibility is to just do you.
Their conduct is none of your business, and it has no bearing on how you live, or the standards you live by.
Just live the way you've agreed and decided to live, and honor their right to do the same.

But, isn't our job as Christians to share the gospel, and pray for people, and lead them in the prayer of salvation?
Yes it is.

When...God...leads...you...to...do...that.

You cannot violate their choice, which is why you have to be led by God in when you talk to people, and in what you say to them. He'll let you know when someone's ready to receive you, whether it's for salvation or just counsel in a situation. And He'll lead you in what to say to them.

If He puts someone on your heart, but doesn't tell you to go talk to them about it, then you simply carry them in prayer until He does release you, if He ever releases YOU to do it. You might be the one to intercede for them. But, He might have someone else who will actually go and speak with them.

So, your only responsibility regarding their life is to do you, let them do them, and let God lead you on when, and how, to do anything more than that. That's it

Well if that's it, what do I do with them in the meantime?

You go out to lunch with them, talk about sports, their kids, invite them to dinner, go see a movie. Live life, get to know them, human to human.
Be the presence of God in their lives constantly salting, fragrancing, loving, and providing light for them. Let your life preach.
Let your life share the gospel.
Let your life and the peace you walk in be an oasis for them.
Let how you treat them, how you inspire them, be what pulls them toward God.

Hold the Standard
Hold what standard?
God's standard.

Now, like I said, we're not the standard or conduct police. But that simply means I'm not going to chase people down or beat them over the head with what God has said. But if they ask me my opinion, or bring me into the conversation,
then whatever comes out of my mouth,

and what they see reflected in my life,
will be in line with the word of God.
That's not something I'll shy away from.

And when I talk to them about it, while I'm holding my standard, I'll do so in a way that respects their right to live however they want to live, regardless of what I think about it. And I'll talk to them in a way that holds them as someone worthy of dignity and of God's best love, regardless of what they're doing; because that's how God loves us.

However, the standard doesn't change.
And how they feel, or what they say, about the standard doesn't change the standard.
Nor does it have any bearing on what I do in pressing to live more and more by that standard. Respecting their choice is where I let them do them.
And holding the standard is where I do me, God's way.

As ambassadors, our main work is to just be, and then to do as we're led. I know we get anxious about whether we're doing enough. But, as we've seen, the metaphors given to illustrate our functions with people are all passive and quiet. Salt disappears into what it contacts. Fragrance dissipates into the air. Light is a facilitator and love is a resolve.

As we go about the business of being amazing artists, we're to publicize the good news of life in Christ. Yes, this is done through our words, but it's much more effective when done first through our actions and evidenced in our lives. St. Francis of Assisi admonishes us to "preach the gospel at all times, and when necessary, use words."

How are we to represent the Kingdom when we interact with people? We display who He is and dispense His goodness as we're led. When people open themselves to deeper conversation, we're to be led by the Spirit in how to proceed. Remember, sometimes we're just there to till the soil of their heart, to break up the hardness that has formed through bad experiences with life, Christians, and the church. Sometimes we're just there to plant the goodness of God in someone's life – through a word of encouragement, by prayer, by sowing into their life, through sharing our connections, time, and resources. Sometimes we're there to water what's already been deposited in them. Then, sometimes we're there to enjoy the privilege of welcoming a new brother or sister into the family.

The third thing we said makes ambassadors effective is that they understand they're in a long-term operation. Relationship is the secret, but time is the necessity. Eccl. 3:1 says, "To everything *there* is a season, A time for every purpose under heaven…" Lk. 8:15 talks about the idea of bearing fruit with patience. It takes time for people to arrive at the place where they're able to see beyond their culture and prejudices, and recognize the value in a different way of being and thinking. It often takes much, much longer than we're usually led to believe when taught about evangelism in church.

Over the summer of 2017, I got to see this in action. Arianna Caligiuri is the founder of Edge Project, a missions program that brings college artists to Spain to experience a convergence of faith, art, and culture. Participants learn how to use their art to demonstrate their faith through serving people of another culture.

There's a pair of brothers she's been carrying in her heart for several years. She prays for them. She patronizes their business and brings them new business year after year. When she's at their restaurant, she always engages them in conversation. This exchange reached a new point in the summer of 2017, where after several years of planting seeds of friendship and prayer behind the scenes, they finally asked her to explain more to them about this Jesus. They didn't say they were yet ready to accept Him as their Lord. But they'd seen enough over the years that they were ready to hear more. She, and the Edge Directors cooked them a meal, shared Jesus with them, and prayed for them.

The point of that story is that Arianna was willing to give the process time. She also was sensitive to the season she was in, in her relationship, and in her individual encounters with them over the years.
Are you willing to give the process time in the lives of the people you encounter? Are you willing to be sensitive to the season of the moments you share with them? In an individual's life, it may only be the season to till the ground, to break up perceptions and prejudices, fears and wounds formed from prior experiences. Perhaps they need time to see someone who says they follow God, actually act like they follow God, and be consistent in their actions for a long period of time.

It may only be the season to plant little seeds - not by quoting scripture, but by being salt, light, fragrance, love, and a good friend.

Maybe you're watering seeds that've previously been sown. Or, maybe it's the time for you to lead that life into a relationship with God through salvation. When we listen to the Holy Spirit, He'll guide us in these times and seasons.

6 **Places, People. Places**

The last thing we said made
ambassadors effective was their
confidence. They know their
government supports them. They know
it has their back. This liberates them to
do what they need to do. As artists in
Christ working in "secular" culture, we need this confidence in two
areas:
1 That we're supposed to be out there in the first place.
2 That we're out there doing what we're supposed to be doing there.

By Mt. 13:37-38 and Jn. 17:15,18, we can be confident that God is in us
being present and active in "secular" culture. We can be even more
confident in the fact that He sends and plants us there; we don't just
drift, wander, or stray there. This is important because it empowers you
to stand flat-footed knowing that your "secular" art career can't be used
to accuse you of falling away from the faith.

Now, to the bigger issue of the two: are you doing what you're supposed
to be doing there?
Not having a definitive answer to this question will absolutely affect
your confidence. It'll not only cheat you out of something God gave
you, but also render you ineffective as an ambassador.

As we jump into this, let's start by admitting that personal career hopes
and dreams can really make things confusing.

Having a gift is one thing. Placing it in a career brings in ambition,
desire, identity, pride, and all kinds of other things that can cloud and
color God's actual path for us. We have to acknowledge that we have a

tendency to embrace assumed paths for our gifts. If we can sing, we assume we're supposed to move to Los Angeles and pursue a record deal. If we do film, we have to knock down doors in Hollywood. If we sing, act, and dance, we think we need to move to New York and pursue Broadway. And on and on. This presents an interesting dilemma for us as artists in Christ, particularly when having to discern whether the career path we're pursuing is our desire, our assumption, someone else's counsel, or God's direction.

Why does this matter?
Because we're talking about confidence.

You can't be confident if you're not once-and-for-all convinced that you're right where God wants you to be, doing what He wants you to do,
particularly in the kinds of careers I'm speaking to.

If you're not settled in that, you can't truly embrace your career because you're still struggling with wondering if God is okay with it.

If you're still struggling with His permission, you won't be able to accept your career as a valid, honorable way to serve Him and live as a Christian.

If you can't accept its validity, you'll struggle to accept that God is in this career journey with you, and that He's pleased with you in it.

If you can't accept His approval, you won't ask Him for what you need. If you're not convinced that He's for you in this journey, you'll feel too conflicted to talk to Him about what you're experiencing.

If you shut Him out of the journey, you'll never experience the fullness of what He intended for you, and through you, as an artist in Christ working in "secular" culture.

If you can't accept your career for what it is and where it exists, then you can't honor it. If you can't honor it, then you certainly can't stand tall in it as being honorable.

If you see no honor in your kind of career and artistry, you'll struggle to embody your place as His ambassador in your career,
which will cut people off from the goodness of God they were supposed to experience through you because you were too wrapped up in shame.

This confidence frees you from feeling conflicted about the form or context of your art life as a person of faith. It frees you from feeling conflicted about the presence of faith as a serious practitioner of art. You can't stand tall in your career if you're conflicted about any of these parts, or their relationship with one another. But, if you're constantly uncertain about how God feels about them, conflict is inevitable.

At one of our Artist Prayer Collective gatherings, the conversation took an interesting turn to careers. To say that there was a collective anxiety, and holding of the breath, is an understatement at best.

What if God tells me that this career path I'm pursuing is not the one He has for me?
This is one of *the scariest* 'what if's' for artists of faith on the career path.

How do I know this is what God wants me to do?
This unanswered question is one of the greatest sources of anxiety for artists of faith on the career path.

For career-minded artists, there tends to be very beaten, generationally-trodden paths. There are well-established career routes people before us have taken with their gift. When we recognize a gift within ourselves, there's the assumption (and leading) that we should take that gift in a particular direction, as those before us have done.

There are basically four ways you can go with career paths.
There's the one people say you should take, the one you assume you should take, the one you really want to take, and the one God has for you.

If you have the golden ticket, all four of these point in the same direction. However, as we all well know, that's hardly ever the case.

So, what to do?

Well, having people advise a career path can be helpful, as the bible says there's wisdom in the multitude of counsel (Prov. 11:14). Their suggestion might highlight something you weren't aware of, steer you in the right direction, or confirm a direction you sensed, but weren't yet confident about.

Desiring a particular career path is also okay; even though Christian culture tends to be really harsh on personal desire and ambition. But, if God gives us the desires of our heart (Ps. 37:4), then desire, in itself, can't be a bad thing. It's how you handle desire, and the place you give it, that can make things kind of hairy.

Assuming you're supposed to take a particular career path just feels silly because you're making decisions on factors that've neither been researched or confirmed. With a little investment of time and research, assumption can very easily become solid decision-making. The assumed path seems like an unwise journey taken for very unavoidable reasons.

In all four of these path possibilities, the jackpot comes in knowing and locking into the one God has for you.

Why, then, do we not always see it as a jackpot?
Where does the anxiety about God's path for our life come from?

Why is it that we want to know God's will for our life, but are simultaneously scared to find out what it is?

I started to tell you about one of our Artist Prayer Collective conversations. During the talk, one woman shared her struggle with the group. Let's call her Alice. Alice had moved to a city to pursue what she believed God was leading her to do. She talked about how discouraged she was because she was experiencing some opposition. Things were taking a long time, and they weren't moving forward as she anticipated they would.

Then she asked, "How do you know when this is what God has for you?"

I recognized a familiar struggle in her story. Difficulty, feeling stagnant, and the passage of time can cause incredible mental freak outs and make us doubt if we ever heard God. They can also make us question why we're still doing what we're doing. I know that place very, very well. I am the tour guide for that place.

I shared my story with her and the group, hoping to show that difficulty, seeming stagnation, and the passage of time are just sucky, unavoidable parts of this walk - not indicators that you missed God.

God told me to go to school for dance. But it took me 12 years to actually get into one. That's 12 years of being told 'no,'
feeling rejected and not good enough,
having to put myself back together again after being rejected,
having to muster up the courage (or insanity) to apply and audition one more time,
failing repeatedly in front of everyone and having to hear them say very hurtful things about me,
looking and being called selfish, irresponsible, in denial, and just downright disillusioned.

My family was actively against what I was doing. They thought I was too smart to be so stupid for so long. They thought I was wasting my life and talent, being unrealistic. And they were very vocal about it in very descriptive language.

I was always broke. I would only take odd jobs to make sure I was available to take class, go on auditions, and take opportunities that were moving me in the direction God was leading me. This might've been sort of acceptable at 19, 20, and 21. But at 24, 25, and 26 years old, I was looking really bad. Many of my friends had finished their Master's, were getting married, going on their second and third child. Many of them were in established careers. And then there was me.

After 12 years of trying to get into dance school, I finally got accepted to the Towson University Dance Department in Maryland. But I was totally broke. I didn't even have money to get to the school, let alone pay for classes and live once I got there. And I was 27 at this point, so there'd be no financial support. Besides, they really didn't want me to go. They thought it was another one of those "Marlita decisions" to even try to go.

All they had seen me do for the past 12 years was struggle, fail repeatedly, and hit one closed door after the other. After 12 years, with virtually no indication that I was moving in the right direction, I was now talking about moving to a place clear across the country where I had no family, no friends, no kind of support whatsoever. Again, I didn't even have money to get there. But I refused to believe that a door would finally open for me to do what God told me to do 12 years ago, only to be unable to walk through it because of something as silly as money. I told my family to just help me get on Maryland soil and God would take care of the rest.

I did get to Maryland.
God did take care of the rest.
I did graduate.
And I've been making a living in dance in various ways ever since.

There was a lot of difficulty in that season. You better believe I often felt frustrated and stagnant. And 12 years felt like forever. It felt like it was never going to happen. But it did. And it still is.

I explained to Alice that in the midst of all this, God's voice was consistent. He sent people into my life at strategic times to encourage me and confirm I was going in the right direction. There was *a lot* of hardship, but there were also obvious wins and progress forward. And every time I got past the discouragement,
every time I got past the negative and sarcastic comments,
every time I actually did what He was leading me to do, there was such joy and peace.
It filled me with life,
every time.

When the Collective had finished, Alice came over to me and we spoke some more about her struggle. I told her to ask God to clarify what He has for her again. Tell Him that things have gotten muddled and that she needs a fresh picture, fresh direction. I've asked for that many times along the way and God has always been faithful to provide it.

She stared at me and her eyes began to tear up. Her expression told me we'd pinpointed the thing she was really afraid of. Her real question wasn't *how do I know if this is what God wants me to do?* Her real question was *what if what I'm doing, or what I've been doing, is not what God has for me?*

How many of you are facing this possibility, and are scared about it?

I told Alice that I understood her fear. But, if she really wanted her 'what-if's' settled, she was going to have to be courageous enough to hear the real answer.

Like Alice, some of you aren't confident about your career because you were led to it by desire, assumption, or counsel,
…and you're hoping that God is in it and/or okay with it,
…and you're terrified to find out where He actually stands on it.

So, you don't ask.
And because you don't ask, you don't know.
And the not knowing destroys your confidence.

If this is you, I need you to be courageous, too. The courage is not needed to hear His answer. The courage is needed for what His answer might make you have to face.

You might have to face the possibility that you were led to this by something other than God, and now you're going to have to change course to get into His will.

You might have to face the sinking feeling that you've wasted time; that all the time you were doing this, you could've been doing the right thing had you just (fill in the blank).

You might have to admit that you were wrong and some of your naysayers were actually right.

You might experience a temporary loss of confidence in your ability to hear God. How could you be so sure and so wrong?

You might have to face the aching of a desire unfulfilled. *I really wanted to do this.*

You might have to face the feeling of your confidence being shaken. *I didn't have what it takes to do this.*

You might have to face your identity being rocked. *I'm nobody if I'm not doing this. If I'm not doing this, who am I?*

You might have to face the agony of feeling like you're settling, as if what God has for you is lesser in quality, or a sub-par plan B.

You might have to face your pride being humbled when you have to explain to people why your plan A didn't work and you're now going in another direction.

You might have to face a change in friendships or a loss in 'status.' God's path for you might not be as sexy or glitzy as the one you're currently pursuing. People tend to leave after that kind of shift.

These are things you might have to face; and the possibility of having to face them is what actually makes you hesitant to check in with God about your career path.

But here's the actual situation:

There's the reality of what you sense, and the package you assume it'll come in.
There's the reality of what you want, and the form you'd like it to take.
There's the real thing, and there's your assumed, or desired, packaging for the real thing.

I liken it to finding a mate. There's what we really want in a mate, and there's the package we hope it all comes in. For example, the package I want is a 6'2," dark chocolate man with a bald head and a muscular build. But what I really want is someone who will love me, support me in doing God's work, someone who won't cheat on me or abuse me, someone with a sense of humor and a zest for life, etc.

Now, what if all the things I actually want aren't found in the 6'2," dark chocolate man with the bald head and muscular build? What if they all come in a 5'11" Latino man with a slender build and receding hairline. Am I settling? Am I missing out? Is he a sub-par plan B?

If I could get over myself and look past the packaging, I'd discover that I was getting all that I actually wanted, even though what I wanted didn't come in the form I thought, or even hoped, it would. I'm going to go out on a limb and propose this is what you're really dealing with.

I believe that you've sensed God correctly about having a career in art. I also believe that you've correctly sensed that your career would be out in "secular" culture. I believe there just needs to be a reconciling between what you *want* your career to look like, and what God has for you. They may end up being the same. And if they're not, God is still one who gives us the desires of our heart. I won't say what He will or won't do.

The bottom line is this: if you haven't had the talk with Him yet, you need to have it.

Here's why:

Whatever it ends up being, your greatest efficacy, your greatest sense of purpose and fulfillment, and your greatest connection to His providence and provision occur when you're in His will for your life. In that place, you'll find all the fulfillment and provision you thought could only be found in the other path. Besides, if we tell the truth, we often find that our dream package ends up being a huge disappointment, anyway.

True confidence requires us to take that very scary look into ourselves and make sure we're not pursuing out of assumption. This can be unbelievably difficult; especially if you really want this, you've been pursuing it for a long time, or you've made a lot of sacrifices to get into it.

If you lay your career before God and discover that He actually has a different direction for you, go ahead and process that. Have your cry, experience your emotions, and give your path it's eulogy and burial. Then, wash your face, straighten your back, and embrace what He has for you because that's where you'll find all the wonderful things you thought the other path was going to give you.

Here's a prayer to help you launch that conversation:

Lord, I recognize that I am gifted to _____. I have desires for this gift. I want to use it in (*kind of career*) to (*what you want to do with it*). However, I acknowledge that You have given me this gift. And I acknowledge that You have desires, plans, and intentions for it. I understand You have reasons for giving it to me. I want to honor You and honor those reasons. So, Lord, I give You my desires, my ambitions, my hopes and dreams for this gift. I don't give them to You because they're bad. You are God who honors our dreams, causes us to hope, and gives us the desires of our heart. Instead, I give them to You because You know the things I truly want. You know my innerworkings. You know what I need. You know what's best for me and I trust that You want what's best for me. I ask You for Your plans for this gift, because I trust that all I actually want is found in following You.

7 Walking the Line

Stepping back out into our larger
conversation, we're talking about
associating with a different culture.
We just finished looking at being a Christian, existing in "secular"
culture and interacting with the people in it. Now, we're going to look
being within that culture without taking it on.

When I was preparing for this chapter, I thought, again, about the
undercover officer. I pictured the one who goes too far. We've all seen
the movie where the officer gets caught up in the life while trying to
take the bad guys down: the one who gets addicted to drugs because
they shoot heroin or sniff cocaine to show they can be trusted and
moved higher up in the cartel.

This is a concern we harbor to varying degrees. What if that happens to
us while we're trying to engage? What if we get caught up out there? I
mean, there's some bad stuff that goes down in the entertainment
industry. Well, shady practices exist no matter what context your art
lives in.

How far do we take this associating business?

In 1 Cor. 9:19-22, Paul shares his way of handling this, which he sums
up in v. 22: "I have become all things to all *men*, that I might by all
means save some."

Um…really?

Actually, in verse 21, he gives us boundaries. He only goes as far as is
within being in right standing with God. We're not to violate the

principles of uprightness before God to win people to God, or to get ahead in the things He's leading us to do.

What kind of sense would that make?

So, we have this issue of associating with "secular" culture without taking on its culture.
How does that work?
How do we keep from crossing the line and getting caught up?
To answer that, we have to clarify what it means, and doesn't mean, to take the culture on.

One principle we've used for guidance is found in 1 Jn. 2:15, which tells us not to love the world or the things in it. And we stop there. But a dilemma arises when we stop there. Let me show you why.

What are the things we usually associate with the world, particularly in artistic and entertainment endeavors?
Financial success
Notoriety and fame
Having a seat at exclusive tables
Accolades and being celebrated for our artistry and excellence, etc.

These are the things we usually associate with the world. And these are the things we believe we shouldn't want or touch because the world wants, and has, them. And this, right here, presents a *particular* dilemma for us as career artists in Christ.

Why?

Well, let's be honest. We love God, and we want to serve and honor Him.
But we're not sacrificing all we are to be poor.
We're not doing it to be obscure and unimpactful.
We're not doing it to be G-list artists.

And, more than that, the vision God activates in us for our art life is one where we're successful in our industry, prosperous in our lives, and fulfilled in our hearts.

So, what gives?

Now, this is definitely something we need to take a moment to deal with. Because we equate such things with "worldliness," we can be unsure, sometimes fearful and suspect, of these aspects of our career life. And we needn't be. There's a difference between "worldliness" and things that happen to also exist in the world. There's a difference between having things and loving them in the 1 Jn. 2:15 way. There's a difference between wanting things and loving them in that way.

Remember that list we made earlier? Those are not things of the world. They're actually covenant blessings. They're all things God says He'll give us when we follow Him. Throughout His word, He says He will:
Make our name great – Gen. 12:1
Prosper the work of our hands – Ps. 90:17
Empower us to get wealth – Deut. 8:18
Cause us to stand before kings and great men – Prov. 18:16
Make us rich – Prov. 10:22
Give us favor with God and man – Prov. 3:4
Teach us to profit – Isai. 48:17

And there are many, many more.
So, these can't be what it means to love the world and the things in it.

If we read on to 1 Jn. 2:16, we find out what this really means: the lust of the flesh, the lust of the eyes, and the pride of life. It's not the world that's the problem. It's the love of it. It's not the things in the world that're the problem. It's the love of them.

Ok, wait! What's the difference?
To understand that, we need to know more about this concept of love.

In Jn. 14:15, 21, and 23, Jesus says if a man loves Him, he'll keep His commandments. In Mt. 6:24, He lets us know "no man can serve two masters; for either he will hate the one, and love the other; or else he will hold to the one, and despise the other. [One] cannot serve God and mammon."

This love that Jesus is speaking of is not about romance or brotherhood. Not here. This love is about devotion, allegiance, and fidelity. This love asks where your loyalty lies, which is demonstrated by who you follow, who you look to, who you believe and trust, and who influences you. See, loving the world, and the things in it, doesn't just mean wanting things they also happen to want. It's more that you want what they want because you believe what they believe about having it. And you get what you want the same way they get it. It's that you follow them.

You do what they do.

You believe what they believe.

You put your trust in the same places they put theirs.

You model yourself after them as a devoted follower, adopting their way of life as your own.

Loving the world is fashioning yourself to its ways, mindset, and values. Loving the things in it is giving your attention and pursuit to the things it reverences.

What are those?

Lust of the flesh.

I do whatever makes me feel good.

I do whatever I feel like doing.

I take what I want because I want it.

I do what I want because I want to.

Lust of the eyes

I want that, and that, and that, and that, and that, and that, oh, and that, too.

It's wanting everything you see because you just want.

What you have is never enough. You always want more. And your life is built around getting more.

Pride of life
I'm a self-sustaining island because I have this money, status, position; because I'm this person,
because I have this relationship, etc.
It's arrogance because of what I have, trusting in those things to protect, sustain, define and fulfill me.

So, taking on "secular" culture has nothing to do with having, or wanting, the same things people in that culture want and have. Instead, it has to do with our *method* of getting those things, the *value* we place on having them, and the *authority* we give them to direct and define our lives. Throughout the Word, we're instructed not to walk in the counsel (Ps. 1:1), the way (Prov. 1:15 / 4:14), or the course (Eph. 2:2) of the world. We're not to pursue the things they pursue in the ways, and for the reasons, they pursue them (Mt. 6:32). We're not to be drawn, motivated, influenced, or guided by the same worldview that leads them.

Let's look at 1 Tim. 6:6-10.

> "Now godliness with contentment is great gain. For we brought nothing into *this* world, *and it is* certain we can carry nothing out. And having food and clothing, with these we shall be content. But [they that will, KJV] be rich fall into temptation and a snare, and *into* many foolish and harmful lusts which drown men in destruction and perdition. For the love of money is a root of all *kinds of* evil, [it is through this craving that, AMP] some have strayed from the faith in their greediness, and pierced themselves through with many sorrows."

1 Tim. 6:10 is incredibly, disrespectfully misquoted. Many people wrongly say money is the root of all evil. That's a lie.

I said that's a lie!!!

There's nothing wrong with wanting financial success and influence. There's nothing wrong with wanting to be at the top of your game. There's nothing wrong with working hard, going for what you know with all your might.

You don't need to feel guilty about wanting, or even working toward, any of that.

You don't have to choose between God and financial success.
You don't have to choose between having a prolific career and serving Him.
Money is not the root of all evil. The *love* of money is the root of all evil.

Again, what's the difference?

Well, for starters, the love of money is not about the money, at all. It's the attitude that says I'll do anything to get and keep it. Now, I know we're specifying money, here; but I believe this is a principle that applies to anything we want— whether it be money, influence, a place in a dance company, an opportunity to work with a particular artist or director, etc. As Christians, we've been reared in an embattled relationship with desire and ambition. But, there's nothing wrong with desire, or with having ambition, when your sufficiency is in Christ. It's one thing to say, *Lord, I really desire to have this, but I'm thankful for all that You've done for me, and I'm fulfilled in our relationship.* It's another matter, entirely, to betray that relationship because you want something and are willing to do anything to get it.

What happened to them?
We've all heard stories and witnessed loved ones who diligently believed God to open doors for them in their industry, only to lose their way in it once they got inside. We've witnessed people change, their hearts harden, their relationships with God stagnate, even diminish, as they continued in their artistic pursuits.

Why does this happen?

How does it happen?

How does one, who was once so fired up for the things of God, change so drastically?

How does the desire to be a light transform into one focused solely on more and more gain?

How does one who has access to life abundantly fall to hustling to maintain?

In Mt. 10:16, Jesus says, "Behold, I send you forth as sheep in the midst of wolves…" The Lord showed me a powerful truth in this verse: Jesus made that statement in the context of telling His disciples how to identify and conduct themselves as they go out on assignment. He tells them to remember that they are sheep. They're not wolves. As they go out, they'll witness and experience actions and methods that are influenced by all kinds of intentions and all manner of ambition. The disciples will be among the wolves, but they're not to think or act like them.

He tells His disciples that they're sheep, and to, therefore, act like sheep: wise and harmless.

The word *wise* means "to be mindful of one's interests (Gr. *Phronimos)*."

The word *harmless* means to "be unmixed in the mind, free from evil or guile, innocent (Gr. *Akeraios)*."

Sheep act one way.

Wolves act another.

Sheep are driven by one thing; wolves another.

As we go out, Jesus instructs that we're not to mix the two. We're to be mindful about our actions and reasons for action, making sure they're not born out of a mixture of desires, intentions, and methods.

When does desire shift from being healthy and benign, to destructive and divisive?

How do we get caught up in our priorities?

Led astray by our ambitions?

Separated into our careers?

We forget that we're sheep…not wolves.

SHEEP	WOLVES
• Thrive in relationship.	• Territorial and competitive
• They prefer to be in communities	• Will kill other wolves if threaten position or food supply
• They are easily satisfied. They just want to eat	• Carnivorous, devours other life to get what it wants
• Not territorial	• Satiate themselves at the expense of others
• Look to be led and are easily led	• Take up more than they need to survive to keep a steady supply of prey
• Have a shepherd to guide them and watch over them	• Travel constantly in search of prey
	• They are ravenous and destructive

As we navigate our careers, we must do so from a place of identity and relationship. The wolves have no shepherd to guide them. No way has been prepared for them, nor place set aside; so, they must fend for themselves. They amass a bigger territory than they need, and kill their competitors out of fear of starving. This is what drives the wolves' actions. But, that's not the nature of our existence in relationship with God.

So, we're not to act like them, as if it was.
We don't need to.
But we also have to make sure we don't become their prey.
How do sheep become wolf prey?
They stray from their shepherd.

When we consider our artistic ambitions outside the context of our relationship with God, we, too, become prey to the wolves of fear (that He won't really be able to make it happen), anxiety (that we'll miss our chance if we don't find a faster way to get it done), worry (that He won't really give it to us), and pride (believing we know a better, easier way to get it done).

I was having fellowship with a group of dancers and the conversation turned to financial success and influence. As we were talking about how these live in the Christian life, one dancer shared the analogy of holding such success with an open hand. This led me to think about an important question each of us have to answer as people of God pursuing careers that, we pray, will include all forms of success.

Why do we want what we want?
Why are we driving so hard to get the career, and achieve the level of success we're pursuing?

While there's nothing wrong with wanting them, our reasons for the desire can get us into trouble if we wrongly imagine what having them will change for us.

> James 1:13-15 (AMP),
> "Let no one say when he is tempted, 'I am tempted by God;' for God cannot be tempted by evil, nor does He Himself tempt anyone. But each one is tempted when he is drawn away by his own desires and enticed. Then, when desire has conceived, it gives birth to sin; and sin, when it is full-grown, brings forth death."

When I was studying this, the Lord brought up Mk. 4:19, which talks about the deceitfulness of riches.

What is that?

The deceitfulness of riches is the mindset towards having a thing, where you believe there's something in it for you that you don't already have;
that having it will solve your problems,
or that it will define and fulfill you in a way you can't experience without it.
Basically, it's what we're convinced will happen by having the thing we desire: what it will give us, or who it will make us. If we're not careful, we can easily find ourselves in this mindset over our career pursuits.

We don't need to look any further than Hollywood or the music industry—at the destruction despite having all the career trappings— to see this is not true in any way.

Eve was tricked by the deceitfulness of riches. She was drawn away by her own desires.
The riches she desired was knowledge and to be like God.
The deceit was that the tree was going to give her something she didn't already have.

She and Adam had full, unhindered communication with God and they were made in His image.
They were already like God.
Yet, in the moment, she lost sight of who she was; and, as James 1:15 says, a desire was birthed in her, which led to the sin of eating from the tree (despite being told not to), and resulted in her and Adam being cast from the garden.

When we separate our career life from our relationship, we become susceptible to the deception that our career has something God can't give us, or is something He's trying to keep away from us; and thus, is something we have to circumvent Him to get.

Another way we can be deceived in desire and ambition is in identity. As artists, it's very easy for us to let our image, our accomplishments, our relevance, and our abilities define us. It's very easy to allow those we respect, and want to work with, tell us who we are, and define the boundaries of our capabilities. We have to be diligent to keep that place reserved for the Father, alone. Otherwise, we open ourselves up to the wolves. As soon as we allow any part of these to define us, we put ourselves on the path to compromise, where we're willing to do anything necessary to maintain the things upon which our identity is formed.

We see this in Mark 10, where Jesus has an encounter with a man who wants to inherit eternal life. The man asks Jesus what he needs to do.

He tells him to follow the Commandments. The man says, *I've done that, been doing that since my youth.*

In the Matthew account, the man then asks Jesus what he's missing? And in Mk. 10:21, the Bible says,

> "Then Jesus, looking at him, loved him and said to him, 'One thing you lack: Go your way, sell whatever you have and give to the poor, and you will have treasure in heaven; and come, take up the cross, and follow Me.' But he [the man] was very sad at this word and went away sorrowful, for he had great possessions. Then Jesus looked around and said to his disciples, 'How hard it is for those who have riches to enter the kingdom of God!' And the disciples were astonished at his words. But Jesus answered again and said to them, 'Children, how hard it is for those who trust in riches to enter the kingdom of God!' It is easier for a camel to go through the eye of a needle than for a rich man to enter the kingdom of God.'"

Now, when we first look at this, it almost seems like Jesus is saying you can't have both; like you can't have riches and enter the kingdom of God. But we know that's not true.

So, what's this about?

The Lord led me to look at this exchange through the lens of identity: where it's defined and rooted. Notice the way Jesus describes the man who will find difficulty entering the kingdom. He doesn't say a man who is rich will have difficulty. He says a rich man will struggle to enter the kingdom.

The difference between these two is huge.

The rich man identifies himself *by* his riches (Prov. 10:15). This is where his confidence comes from, his sense of place, his sense of relevance, of security and safety. He's wrapped up in all that being rich gives him—emotionally, socially, in terms of access, etc. To this man, his riches are the source and reason for all the good he experiences in his life. Without them, there is no "him." Since his riches are crucial to his identity, he has to do whatever's necessary to keep them, even walk away from Jesus.

As soon as we allow any part of our ability or career to define us, we put ourselves on the path to compromise, where we're willing to do anything necessary to maintain the things upon which our identity is formed.

We can fall into this with our career, or with the gift, itself. I was watching a documentary on Whitney Houston, and one of the people interviewed said, "Whitney is her voice." That really struck me hard—particularly considering all the damage that thinking did in her life. Houston did drugs for many reasons, I'm sure. Among those, she did them to keep her going when she was exhausted, when she should've said no, and taken a break. But how can you do that when you *are* your voice?

How many artists have we seen struggle, fall into depression, unable to appreciate being still for a season, because they battle the thought: Who am I if I'm not doing this?
Or, what about those who fear losing all the benefits of success when they're not at the top anymore?
What is their value as a person without them?
And because their identity is built on the status of their gift and career, they feel they have to do whatever it takes to maintain them, even things they never imagined they'd do.

So, why do you want what you want?

As we think about existing in "secular" culture as Christians, we're really asking how we engage without adopting its worldview about what we want, the reasons we want it, and the way we go about getting it.

That begs another question: Where, and how, does God factor into the world of our desire and ambition? Being in the world, but not of it, makes you have to think about how you end up being of it. And that boils down to trust.
If you don't trust that God is able and willing to help you achieve your career ambitions, you won't follow Him in getting them.
You won't even consider Him.
In fact, you'll be willing to exclude, even circumvent, Him to accomplish them, which is exactly what "secular" culture does. You'll find yourself more willing to do things you don't necessarily want to do, but believe you have to do, to get where you're going because that's the only option you believe you have to get there.

Not all of us will face such dire dilemmas, but opportunities to do things the non-God way will be plenty; and compromising is way easier than we want to think.

Now, some might say I'm naïve, ignorant, too idealistic in saying this:
but if God is the source and director of your art life,
if He's the one who exalts you,
if He's the one who gives you favor and sets divine appointments and relationships,
if He's the one who finishes what He starts in your life
you don't have to give in to such dilemmas to get where it's in your heart to go.

You don't have to smoke the weed that's being passed around the table just because the director's passing it around; where you're hoping that by smoking it with everyone else, you'll get invited to the next party and, eventually, invited to join the team.

You don't have to do that.

Being in the world, but not of it, is not about drinking and drugs, too much money or success. It's about *how* you become of it.

Others might say, *Marlita, this whole chapter is talking about what we want, not about serving God. The focus should be on Him, not our wants.* Well, my friend, I lovingly push back by pointing out that they're not mutually exclusive. Actually, they're very much related. If you look at Mk. 4:19 and 1 Tim. 6:6-10, the whole reason we get drawn away is because of what we want and the hopes we attach to receiving it.

The reason we struggle to choose God, to choose His way in a situation, is because of the fear of our wants never being fulfilled if we do.

So we have to talk about what we want.

We can't just ignore desire, want, and ambition because we're Christians. We can't shun them as bad because God fulfills them.

Here's the deal:

In many ways, being in, but not of, the world boils down to how you manage wanting, desiring, and having ambition.

The world manages it one way. The Spirit of God leads you to handle it in another way.

The world goes after want one way. The Spirit of God fulfills it another way.

The world attributes a certain value to having them. The Spirit of God attributes another, entirely.

The only true way to be active in "secular" culture without adopting it, is to invite God into the space of your want,

to lay it at His feet,

allow Him to journey in it with you,

and lead you in it. The only other way to be is as one who keeps Him out of that space, and to get things the way those who keep Him out of that space get them. It's only one or the other.

It lies in rooting your identity in who He says you are.

It lies in holding yourself accountable for remembering who your source is.

He's the one who fulfills all your needs and desires.

He fills the holes.

He grants the peace.

He gives the sense of importance.

He opens the doors no man can shut.

He brings your gift in front of great men.

He causes people to favor you.

So, pursue God.

Find contentment in Him, and determine that what makes you enough is Him.

Do that, and you'll have the desires of your heart.

What we've just finished discussing is what it means to take on "secular" culture, which we're not to do. But, we are supposed to participate in it.

What does that look like?

When I was thinking about this, the concept of assimilation came to mind. As I looked into this, I found there are at least three things that happen when one culture enters another: either they merge (assimilation), intersect (acculturation), or coexist.

Merge: In assimilation, the minority merges into the new culture, losing the original features of their own culture. This can happen to the point where the two cultures can no longer be distinguished apart from one another.

Intersect: In acculturation, people retain the majority of their original culture, but adapt it by taking on aspects of the larger culture.

Coexist: The minority culture lives amongst the majority culture but rigidly maintains all aspects of its culture that were present before contact.

Adopting certain practices that are standard in "secular" culture is not necessarily a bad thing. We know the line we can't cross in this, which is the point at which it violates God's word. We know that we aren't to be led and drawn by the same mindset. But, if we're honest, there are plenty of ways we take on parts of "secular" culture as artists in our career life.

Merging example

God leads you to pursue a career as a recording artist. The established culture for musicians is that you have to have a demo tape made before anyone will even consider you. Or, if you're working to be an actor, the established protocol for auditioning actors is that you have to have a headshot. This is the established protocol in your career culture, even though it's not in your faith culture.

But you assimilate.

It doesn't compromise your faith to follow that cultural practice of getting headshots or demos made.

Again, we have to remember we are guests. How do we be gracious guests?

In Spain, I get such a different reaction from people when I speak their language, than when I speak English. Even when I'm fumbling for words, they engage with me differently. They help me. They teach me the right way to say it, and congratulate me when I get it right. We chuckle and a tiny moment of bonding occurs. Even though it takes me longer to speak to them in Spanish, they're willing to wait because they appreciate my willingness to honor and participate in their culture. They appreciate my recognition that I'm a guest in their home and am working to follow the customs they practice there.

What's the biggest complaint about Christian artists? Well, there are several. But, the complaints are rooted in a lack of appreciation for the values held by the art community in the culture we're entering, like excellent craftmanship.
Jesus said, "Render unto Caesar what is Caesar's..." (Mk. 12:17). Another saying is *When in Rome, do as the Romans do."* If it's not violating God's word, follow the protocol. Engage in the cultural practice.

Intersect example

It may be the established protocol for you to get headshots done, but you maintain your faith culture while adapting to aspects of "secular" career culture. In your faith culture, you pray and seek the Lord before you make decisions. These two cultures intersect when you seek the Lord about the photographer you should work with for your shots. All recording artists need a demo tape, and you fall in line with that. But, you maintain your faith culture by praying over the session musicians you should work with, the engineer, what songs you should include on the demo, etc.

Coexist example

Artists are always looking for ways to maintain a creative edge. Some of those practices are harmful, but it's believed that they're helpful for creativity. So that becomes the accepted practice. You have another way. They do them. You do you.

Sometimes, this can be really hairy for us as people of faith. Again, we don't want to compromise our faith, or be seen as compromising. So, we spend a lot of energy trying to find out which one of these interactions we should stick to. But, the truth is it will be different from situation to situation. My examples were very broad because the Holy Spirit will lead you in the individual situations and circumstances.

Remember, each of us exists in different contexts. And the liberty we have in Christ is to follow His word as is suitable for the context in which He's placed us. What may be obedience to God in one art career may be disobedience in another.

The best thing I could tell you for engaging in the practices of "secular" culture is to learn how to hear the voice of God. Make hearing Him your highest priority. He will lead you every step of the way, without fear, without condemnation, without having to fit into some "Christian" mold. God will lead you in the tailor-made life He's crafted just for you.

Liberty

+

harmony

=

an art life
with apology

8 It's All in the Eyes

Up until this point, we've been making the case that any art life can serve, build, and represent the Kingdom. That includes your kind of art life, even in what you make art about, the people you make it with, and where you make it.

Our goal is for you to be free to do the art God is leading you to do, without apology. In order to have that, we said you have to have liberty and harmony.

We just dealt with the liberty part of the equation, by which we aimed to release you from the weight of presumptive views on what a Christian's art life should look like. Now we're going to turn the focus inward, as we move to the harmony part of the equation.

Where liberty was about you being able to account for God's hand in your art life, harmony is about the mechanics of your faith, art, and career actually working together.

When I say harmony, what do I mean? Here's the KAI definition:
Harmony is where all parts of yourself, (as a Christian, creative, and cultural participant), are accepted and honored, working together in agreement with God. It's where all three parts are allowed full expression, and are allowed to work together and thrive - all at the same time, in the same space, without apology.

It's a settledness where you experience no conflict, no hesitation, no flee-reflex about being all three at the same time, all the time, in the

121

same space.

It's a confidence, where you stand flat-footed in the full assurance that God is with you, and is pleased with your art life in "secular" culture.

That's a beautiful notion.

But why isn't this unapologetic, effortless, reciprocal collaboration a reality in most of our relationships between faith and career? Why aren't they existing in harmony?
The reason is more than other's ideas of what our art life should look like.
It's more than the fact that we haven't really been taught how to have such a relationship.

At specific times in KAI intensives, I pose the same question to artists in different ways to help them unearth the answer. Essentially, the question is *why aren't your faith, art, and career working together to the degree you want?* Another way I've asked this question is *what are you trying to preserve and avoid by keeping them separate?* We'll unpack that version later. Right now, though, I want to look at this version: What are the hindrances to bringing them together?

When thinking about this idea of harmony, the Lord gave me the image of pruning. Pruning involves removing dead, diseased, and decayed parts of a tree to facilitate its growth. It also involves removing weak parts of the tree that are prone to damage. He posed this question to me: Does pruning the tree cause it to grow? The answer is no. Pruning does not make the tree grow. The tree already has the natural capacity to grow, and it *will* grow as long as nothing is hindering it from growing. Pruning removes the hindrances so the tree can do what is natural for it to do.

In the same way, harmony is a natural process within us. In God, harmony will happen in our lives as long as there is nothing hindering it from happening. The problem with us experiencing harmony is that there *are* things hindering this natural process from progressing within us.

Artist of faith
Artist who is Christian
Artist who happens to be Christian

All of these are labels that I've heard used by Christ-following artists working in "secular" culture to describe themselves. Now, let's be clear: I don't care how you describe yourself. It really doesn't matter to me. But, I am interested in the order of the words used in the describing. And, I'm also interested in the reason behind the order of the words used in the describing.
Why?
Because I think they reveal something.
I think they reveal a fight for preservation,
a distrust, or inability to feel completely safe,
a conflict between two things, where neither one can be fully chosen, and neither can be eliminated,
a split in one who's not convinced that their faith and their life in art can live and fully thrive together in the same space,
a struggle in one who feels like one part of themselves must be sacrificed for the other part to live,
a wrestling in one who feels like one part of themselves doesn't match the standards of acceptability held by the other part.
They reveal things we've been taught, things we've seen and experienced. They also reveal things we've accepted, assumed, and concluded.

In all this, there's actually just one hindrance: perception.

As career-minded artists, we struggle with carrying divisive, unfruitful beliefs about the relationship between our faith and art career. This is understandable after seeing all the opinions and expectations we have to navigate. Regardless of the reason, the beliefs create the hindrance, which have to be pruned so harmony can thrive. To remove the hindrance, we have to tackle the beliefs.

There is no hindrance separating our faith and art career. We only have to address our hindering beliefs and perceptions.

Well, what are they?
What are these beliefs we hold that are making an effortless collaboration difficult?
Our faith and art lives are going in separate directions
One must be sacrificed for the other
Our faith and art career intersect

Ships passing in the night

Some of us see our faith and art lives as divergent, going in separate directions. This belief limits the possibilities of bringing them together. However, we were built for both.
But we don't believe we can have both.
So, we put ourselves in positions where we have to choose.
Yet, we can't choose because we were built for both.
Instead, we make acrobatic accommodations and weather internal conflicts to have as much of both in our lives as possible, even if it's tumultuous and compromised.

This produces an unfortunate result.

We end up spending so much time moving horizontally between the two, that we never make any true progress forward, or find true fulfillment, in either one. All of our emotional, mental, and spiritual energy is spent trying to make a choice and justify the choice we made. We choose one, then feel guilty about the one we chose. Or, we choose one and lament over the one we didn't choose, which takes our focus from the one we did choose. We make the decision to pursue our career and things go well. Yet, we believe we can't have both, and we step away from our relationship with God because we don't want to be hypocritical or disrespectful. So, even though we're progressing in our career, we can't fully enjoy it because we feel the void of our relationship with God.

Or,

We decide to focus on our relationship. But, He built us to engage in our gift. So, though our relationship is growing, we feel the ache of our gift lying dormant. We aren't walking in wholeness because there's an entire facet of ourselves we're not engaging. Basically, any progress made is bittersweet. It's never truly fulfilling because we feel the absence of the one we didn't choose, guilty over the one we did, and embattled about letting them anywhere near each other.

artist

art

The dreaded sacrifice

One day, I posted what I thought was a word of encouragement to artists in a Facebook group. Within my message, I used the term

"Christian artist." Now, I'd heard of the scandal around using that phrase in communities of professional artists; but, I thought that my intentions would be clear in the context of my message. I used it in the most benign sense and it seemed like the most efficient reference. After all, these were artists that I was speaking to, and they were Christians.

I have to tell you: my eyes were opened that day. Nothing else that I said in my message was noticed. All of the responses were about that term - *Christian artist*. They were rapid and fiery, each artist's response explaining to me the error of my word choice in referring to them.

Why the big deal?
They were just a couple of words, right?
Actually, no.

What I totally underestimated, in my naivete, was the long-standing, battleground narrative between the Christian identity and the art career. Through direct declaration, or by implication from things unsaid or left out of favorable conversation, Christians have been cultured to have an embattled view of their career in "secular" culture.

I imagine it to be like the situation between Black women and their natural hair. It's something you have. It's part of you. It's not going anywhere. But for the longest time, Black women were not taught, or supported, in loving their hair, valuing it, or seeing it as a positive, beautiful part of who they were. Many times, they were directly told how undesirable it was. The same has happened with Christians with "secular" art careers. They haven't been taught how to see their art career as a positive, contributing, valuable part of their faith life.

So, like Black women who've struggled to embrace their natural hair, because of the negativity associated with it, Christians have struggled to reconcile their art careers.

To the artists in that Facebook group, and many others, the reference, *Christian artist*, is a kind of taunting, effortlessly partnering two words that represent two parts of themselves they've never yet been allowed to bring together with that same assuming casualness.

To address this, I've seen artists use a spectrum of labels in attempt to reconcile their place and role in this faith / art / career balance.
Think about how you see yourself.
How do you describe yourself to people as an artist in Christ working in "secular" culture?
What struggles come up for you in trying to find the right words to use?

You are an artist.
You're a son of God (not referring to gender, but relationship and position).
And, you're on a particular career path with your art.

Each of these are such strong parts of how you express your *are-ness,* and how you interact and make space for yourself in the world. When you represent yourself in words, you want to use those that honor all parts of who you are as an artist in Christ.

Why?

The way we identify ourselves in this balance is about more than what we do. It also reveals what we value, what we're trying to avoid and preserve, and where our sense of responsibility lies. The placement of the words "artist" and "Christian," and the connective phrasing we put around them, reveal how we see ourselves, and the part of us that most guides our thoughts and actions.

As Christians, our art life should be guided by our faith, which I believe we all know and agree with. However, that becomes difficult when it seems that faith's guidance disregards, or belittles, the other aspects of our *are-ness.*
Going back to the natural hair example, Black women have long been told their hair would only be acceptable and considered beautiful if it were altered – usually by straightening it, making it longer with

extensions, or covering it up altogether and wearing a completely different hair texture with a weave or wig. In the same way, many artists have been told, or left to believe, that the only way their art career would be acceptable was by altering it – either by making it fit into the four church priorities or laying it down altogether.

Hence, the dreaded sacrifice.

During a KAI session, one participant brought up the celebration of martyrdom in the church. I'm sure you've come in contact with this ideology at some point: which says the greatest way to serve and honor God is to martyr yourself and every remnant of your desire, personality, character, and gifting. The problem I have with this thinking is that God built you that way. I understand submitting all parts of yourself to Him to allow Him to properly orient them in His will. I understand submitting all of yourself to His cleansing fire to allow Him to burn away all the unproductive, unfruitful parts of you. But to ask for the whole thing to go up in smoke is ridiculous. He gave you all of that to use to participate in this life in relationship with Him. Your art is not just something you use in Christian service or for your career. Your art is part of how God has given you to engage during your time in this earth.

It's neither necessary, then, to sacrifice your career on the altar, or alter it to be anything other than what God made it.

Giving up something He gave you, or changing it, is not what He's asking you for – unless He's explicitly asked you to do that in plain, clear, and specific language. He may redirect you in how you're using your art, to align it with the reason He gave it to you. He may lead you to put it down for a season so He can develop other parts of you necessary for the larger picture of what He has for you. But He's not going to tell you to disconnect from it entirely. Why would He? It's just as much a part of you as your hair and eye color.

Separateness is the problem

One day I was sitting on my bed after just getting out of the shower. I was staring off into space, as was my early morning custom, trying to muster up the strength to go teach 200 restless high schoolers. The Lord interrupted my pouting and said, "Remove the 'and.' It's a derivative relationship, not a dualistic one."

That was it.

That was all He said.

Random, right?

Not really, because I was in the middle of writing an essay about the Christian/Artist duality; so, I knew exactly what He was referencing. I'll be honest, though: I knew what He was referencing, but I didn't really know what it meant. But, I've learned how He speaks to me, and I knew further information would come when I went to look these words up. So, I did.

Basically, seeing ourselves as separate parts is what's causing the problem in the first place. If we have separate parts, we have to spend time and energy negotiating their interaction, and determining the grounds upon which they can interact.

I was at a gathering with some students from Pasadena Art Center. It was a wonderful time of fellowship. At the end of the gathering, our host asked each of the students how we could be praying for them. One student, let's call her Remi, asked us to keep her in prayer about God being #1 in her life. With the demands of art school, and her having a one-track-mind personality (her words), she was struggling to maintain her relationship with God. Her prayer request piqued my interest; so much that I got up to get my notebook so I could write it down. At first, I wrote it down as a question:

What does keeping God first look like in times of busyness and high demand in our career life?

As I was thinking about that, another question came to mind:

What does God being #1 mean to her? What does it mean to any of us?

My initial hypothesis was that it meant Him being front of mind. The Lord then took that thought and led me down another train of thought, where He cut to the heart of the matter.

The perception is that our faith life is separate from our art life. The logic that follows is that we have to leave, or put down, our art to go spend time with God. The problem with that is, in times of busyness and high demand, we don't have "the time" to put our art down and step away because there are people waiting on us to finish and deliver.

So, what happens?

The people waiting for us are tangible, visceral, most immediate. And there are immediate consequences to not delivering, not finishing a project for school, or not meeting the deadline for a launch. We've made our faith and art lives separate, forcing ourselves to have to choose between them.
So, now we have to choose.
And, typically, we choose the one that screams the loudest, the one that renders the feedback we're most accustomed to regarding;
putting our time with God on the backburner.

Now, the prayer for any career-minded artist is that we stay in demand, which means we fall into a flow where we're always choosing our career over God. It means we're always choosing to spend our time meeting a deadline, or hustling on a project, over nurturing our relationship.
And what happens?
The relationship suffers.
We feel distant from God, like we're failing Him. That feeling compromises our confidence in the relationship, causing us to approach Him like He has a whip in His hand; if we go to Him at all.
We punish ourselves, beat our chests, and loathe our selfish and terrible priorities.

The crazy thing about all this is it doesn't have to be this way. It only has to be this way if your art and faith are separate. But they're not, at least not from God's perspective.

The reality is your art life is in God, and God is in your art life. More than that, He's ever-present with you. And more than *that*, He's in you!

He's *in* you!

If He's in you, where do you have to go?
If He's in you, and in your art life, you don't have to leave your art to go to Him.
He's already there.
You only need to acknowledge that He's there and release Him to participate in the fabric, rhythm, practice, conversation, and management of your art life. Your career is a lab, playground, a practice center for your faith. It's a place to put your faith to work; a place where your relationship with God gets to take form on flesh and bone, substance and matter.
But they are not separate.
Your faith is not separate from your "secular" art career.

In fact, I'm going to be bold and just share that I don't believe there is such a thing as "secular" for the child of God, which is why I have it in quotes throughout the book. Here's why:

> Col. 1:16
> "For by Him all things were created that are in heaven and that are on earth, visible and invisible, whether thrones or dominions or principalities or powers. All things were created through Him and for Him."

> Jn. 1:3
> "All things were made through Him, and without Him nothing was made that was made."

Ps. 24:1
"The earth is the Lord's, and all its fullness, The world and those who dwell therein."

Mt. 13:37-38
"He answered and said to them: 'He who sows the good seed is the Son of Man. The field is the world, the good seeds are the sons of the kingdom, but the tares are the sons of the wicked one.'"

Lk. 17:21 (KJV)
"Neither shall they say, 'Lo here! or, lo there!' for, behold, the kingdom of God is within you."

Now, if these scriptures are true, how can anything be "secular" for the child of God:
whose Dad made and owns everything,
who was sown into the world by God, Himself,
and who is the host and carrier of the very Kingdom and presence of God?

How can anything be "secular" if God is mobile within us, and omnipresent in Himself?

And if nothing can be "secular" for the child of God, how can anything be "secular" in a Christian's art career? And if there's nothing "secular" about your art career, how can it be separate from Him?

Now, we can choose to disregard God's principles and participate in elements of worldliness, like worldly and carnal ways, mindsets, pleasures, desires, actions, works, etc. But, to me, that's very different from the concept of the "secular" existence. I see that as something totally different than outright darkness and disregard for uprightness. "Secular" is a context, more akin to locale and orientation; as opposed to an action or state of will.

What does this mean for us in this conversation?

There's nothing our art cannot talk about. It's not what we talk about. It's the perspective we take *on* what we talk about.

There's no place our art can't go. The Lord, Himself, sows us into the world and everything in it belongs to Him.

There's no person with whom we cannot collaborate. We carry the very Kingdom and presence of God with us into every place and encounter. And, we're to be salt (Mt 5:13), light (Mt. 5:14), fragrance (2 Cor. 2:14), and love to those around us. How can we do that if we refuse to interact with them?

We're in the specific conversation about hindrances to bringing our faith and "secular" art career together. We said there was really only one hindrance: internal perception. One of those internal perceptions is the belief that we have to sacrifice our art career on the altar for our faith. That's only necessary if you believe that the *Christian* and *artist* part of you are separate, that you exist as a duality. However, I shared with you what the Lord told me: It's not a dualistic relationship. We're not two separate parts as an artist in Christ. It's a derivative relationship.

What does that mean?

Basically, when we get saved, our relationship with God cocoons and envelops every aspect of our life. From our 'yes' forward, we're to engage in them from the place of relationship. Our art life is also housed within that relationship, and is to spring forth out of it. Our artistry is a way we give expression to our life in God. That doesn't mean always talking about Him.
It's more about conversing with life from a worldview influenced by Him.
It's about reflecting the new ways of seeing and thinking He's opened to us.
It's also about conducting ourselves in a manner influenced by what we learn from Him. Our career is one way we express and apply what we experience within that relationship.

I can totally understand why any artist in Christ would think they had to sacrifice their art career for their faith. I also understand why that fear would cause an artist to keep them apart in a desperate attempt to keep them both alive. Thankfully, the sacrifice is not necessary; again, unless God specifically asks you to do that in clear and plain language.

Going back to my natural hair example, Black women eventually embraced the notion that natural hair and beautiful, long, healthy hair were not in an either/or conflict. They could have both. Beautiful, healthy hair comes out of natural hair once you know what to do with it. Once they were taught how to take care of *their* hair texture, and once they were taught how to style and manage it, there was an explosion of fabulously thick and healthy tresses being sported by Black women down their back. I'm one of them.

In the same way, as Christians with "secular" art careers, our faith and career are not in an either/or conflict. Our artistry and career come out of our faith.

Yes, even our kind of career.

In this conversation, we're learning how to re-imagine and re-orient our faith, art, and career in that reality.

The Mother of all Perceptions

Now, all of these beliefs become a non-factor by addressing our perception about one major thing. And, the fact that they were ever present reveals our struggle with how we've been perceiving this one major thing.
What is that thing?
Our relationship with God.

Again, we're in a conversation about harmony, about getting our faith, art, and career working together in an effortless, reciprocal partnership. When honestly uncovering why we're not experiencing harmony, we find that it's real root lies in the relationship we think we have with God.

Why there?

Because that's where the moment that changed everything lives.

What moment?

The moment you said 'yes.'

You see, your 'yes' changed everything.

Think about it: Had you not said yes, you wouldn't be in *this* conversation pondering how to make the various parts of your life work together with that 'yes.' The fact that you're seeking to build harmony means that, fundamentally, you and God have different ideas about your 'yes,' and about the way things exist since, and because of, your 'yes.' You have different mindsets about your relationship with one another, trying to live a life together in two different directions. And because this divergence exists around the basics of your relationship, you struggle to understand how everything else fits within it, including your art life.

Romans 12:2 talks about being transformed by the renewing, or the renovating, of our minds. Renovation includes rearranging. There's a practice called Feng Shui, which is about arranging the objects in your house for the optimal flow of energy. For us, our understanding of the relationship between faith, art, and career needs to be rearranged for optimal flow of the Spirit of God throughout all these parts of our life. We also need to rearrange some of the ways we think about God, our relationship with Him, and our art life within that relationship. That optimal flow is achieved by placing faith at the head.

Life on the other side of 'yes.'

We said that harmony was about accepting and honoring the function and contribution of each member in the partnership. What, then, is faith's place and role among our art and career? How do we honor it in the way we exist as artists and traverse our career?

We talked about your 'yes,' and about the reality of that 'yes' having changed everything. Everything includes your art life. How you live as an artist, what drives you, what influences your decisions, how you execute career plans and achieve ambitions – these all have a new orientation, a new catalyst. Part of your 'yes' at salvation was an accepting of faith's role as the pilot who would now lead and direct your life, including the course of your artistry and career life, into the things God has for you.

At its most fundamental level, experiencing harmony between faith, art, and career is about embracing and aligning yourself in this new reality on the other side of your 'yes.'

How do we honor faith in the way we exist as artists and traverse our career? God's invitation to us was one into a life lived in, by, and for faith. When I speak of faith, I'm referring to something specific: the environment, or ecosystem, of the faith life. This environment is made up of a social and structural part, like a family. The social part is the relationships: Mom, Dad, sister, brother. The structural part consists of the principles that govern how things get done in the environment. If you need to go somewhere, you ask Dad. If you need something from the store, you ask Mom. If you need to switch chore days, you need to ask your little sister because your big sister won't budge. There are relationships and there are rules of transaction among those relationships. These make up the environment.

In the same way, faith has an environment with a social and structural part. The social part is our relationship with God. The structural part is all the principles that govern how things get done within the relationship.

So, to honor faith is to honor our relationship with God, and the principles of transaction in that relationship, in our creative process and career actions.

What does that look like?

I want to answer that by looking at the social facet of the faith environment first.

Why?

Well, I'll answer that question with a question:

Why do you easily take the advice of one person and reject that of another?

In our KAI workshops, some of the answers to this question have been: because of what we know about the person, our experience with them, and our perception of them. The same goes with God. See, we can't get into governing principles before we address our perception of the person. The principles come from the person. And if you don't trust the person, you won't regard the principles. Think about anarchists. They're anarchists because they fundamentally distrust the government and don't see how they can cooperate with someone they distrust.

Said another way: Your image of who God is, and your understanding of the dynamic between you, has direct impact on how involved you'll allow Him to be in your art life. Your image of Him already affects your ability to relate to Him and give Him access to things that are most precious to you. That's something for each of us to pause and really think about!

> **Your image of who God is, and your understanding of the dynamic between you, has direct impact on how involved you'll allow Him to be in your art life.**

We said before that the lack of harmony, we experience, has its root in our relationship with God. But really, the root is in our understanding of our relationship with Him. It's so cliché to even say it, but, we have some Daddy issues to resolve. Sometimes, the most difficult thing about relationship with God is that our only frame of reference for relationship is our experience relating to other humans. And if we're not careful, we take some of the "lessons" we've learned in relating to other people, and project them onto our relationship with God – where we potentially fall into making constructed assumptions and drawing erroneous conclusions about how to interact with Him.

If our perception affects the way we relate to God, we have to be open to the possibility that we're interacting with a constructed image of Him, instead of who He really is. Further, we have to be willing to open ourselves to more experiences with Him, so that our understanding can be constructed in the truth of who He is.

Since our frame of reference for relationship comes from our interactions with other people, I'm going to lead you through four fictional scenarios. Each of these four scenarios gives us insight into our current experience with harmony. Each of them show how our relationship with God impacts our ability to fully honor faith's place in our career life. After each scenario, I'm going to give you a question to consider and point out some important things to note.

Scenario #1

Renee and Trevor have been together for two years. In those two years, they've gone on many dates, but tonight is special. They finish their meal, and as the plates are cleared, Trevor nervously slinks out of his chair and gets down on one knee before Renee. He looks up at the love of his life and, with his heart pounding, he asks her *Will you marry me?* With tears in her eyes, heart pounding, she answers *Yes! Oh my God, yes!* Months go by as they do all the engagement to-do's. At their wedding, they confirm their proposal and acceptance with their "I do's." Three years later, the marriage breaks down.

Consider: What causes the marriage to break down, even though there was a proposal, a yes, and confirming I Do's?

9 I Do! To What, Exactly?

From the proposal to the exchanging of the marriage vows, these two people were not just looking at each other saying *will you marry me, yes, I will marry you,* and *I do.* Though those were the only words spoken between them, that was not all that was being communicated between them.

When the man looked up at his future wife and asked her to marry him, he was actually saying *I know who you are. I know what you expect of me and of this relationship. I know what comes with you, and I'm saying 'yes.' I accept all of it, and I will be a part of that with you. I take it. All of it.*

As the woman looked at the man she'd be spending the rest of her life with and agreed to marry him, she was actually saying *I know who you are. I know what you expect of me and of this relationship. I know what comes with you, and I'm saying 'yes.' I accept all of it, and I will be a part of that with you. I take it. All of it.*

And this sentiment was confirmed by their wedding *I do's.*

This is the reality of what was being communicated between them. Yet, there are still times when couples fail to recognize the gravity of what their yes is actually saying to one another. Thus, problems arise. And they usually arise for several reasons:

They don't realize that saying yes is saying yes to all that comes with the other person.
They don't realize that saying yes is saying yes to all the changes and adjustments that have to come by being with them.
They say yes, but they don't know all they're saying yes to.

They say yes, but they really didn't mean yes *to all*, and they didn't work that out before they said yes.
They said yes, but for whatever reason, have now decided that they're no longer going to honor their yes.

Regardless of the reason, each partner's yes was pregnant with expectations, hopes, and desires. This is like our relationship with God. His invitation to us was pregnant with expectations, hopes, and desires. And, our yes to His invitation was pregnant with the same.

Think about it:
Why did God invite you into relationship with Him in the first place?
What does He want from you, in you, through you, with you?
And where does your career life fit in His reasons for inviting you into relationship?

Also,

When you accepted God's invitation to relationship, what did you say yes to?
Or, more importantly, what did you *think* you were saying yes to?
And where does your career life fit in your 'yes?'

Part of walking together is reconciling expectations. Remember when I said you and God have different ideas about your 'yes,' and about the way things exist since, and because of, your 'yes?'
This is what I was talking about.
You see, the questions you have to consider about you and God is:
Are we seeing the same things about our relationship with one another?
Are we moving in the same direction?

When these are left unreconciled, problems and stagnation arise because two people are trying to exist in one relationship while moving in two different directions.

Harmony between faith, art, and career means addressing two visions of this relationship between you and God. Having them partner effortlessly requires you to reconcile expectations as a person of faith with expectations as an artist. This reconciliation happens in honest, vulnerable conversations with God about how these components live and work together in your life.

Again, God's invitation to you was pregnant with expectation of how you'd be together in relationship. And, your acceptance of His invitation was also pregnant with expectation of how you'd be together in relationship. In this, you have to pause for a moment of honesty and acknowledge that your expectations tend to come with parameters that protect you in the things you want to preserve and avoid as you relate to Him.

When discussing this scenario in one of our KAI workshops, one participant, Matt, shared two questions his friend told him each person in a relationship must consider about their partner: *Do I want to weave my life into theirs and co-create this new life with them? Do I want to sacrifice part of my own space, routine, and rhythm to align with theirs?*

These are precisely the issues before us in our relationship with God. Are we willing to do away with more and more of our parameters as we feel safer with God and His intentions for us?
Do we understand His intentions for us?
Do we understand where our art life fits within those intentions?

Let's look more into His expectations for relationship with us.

> 2 Cor. 5:15
> "And He died for all, that those who live should no longer live for themselves, but for Him who died for them and rose again."

This is a concept that makes professional artists of faith really nervous: Living for God.

What does that mean?

The idea of living for God, although exciting and desirable in theory, becomes scary in practice when we lose sight of the fact that the career life we envision was given to us by Him in the first place.

If I live for Him, what happens to my art career? Will I have to leave my career and become a missionary for poor children in a remote village in Uruguay? Will I lose creative control? Will I lose directional control over my art and career trajectory? Does this mean that I won't get to experience the career life for which I've worked so hard?
Will I still have the freedom to create art about whatever subjects inspire me?
Will I still be allowed to engage in, and present my art in various contexts? Or can I now only make art for the church?
Can I still collaborate with non-Christians without being judged or disappointing God?

The idea of living for God, although exciting and desirable in theory, becomes scary in practice when we lose sight of the fact that the career life we envision was given to us by Him in the first place. It becomes difficult when we don't recognize that living for Him doesn't take us away from the career vision He's planted in us. Instead, it actually shows us how to get all the way into it. We know our artistic gifts come from Him. Yet, when it comes to our career life, we imagine Him as The Reckoner, coming to take back what was stolen from Him, and we are the thief. But as career artists in Christ, we have to think about living for God while taking into account that He's placed us in "secular" culture to both enjoy pursuing an art career, and be an agent and ambassador while we do it.

2 Cor. 6:16
"And what agreement has the temple of God with idols?
For you are the temple of the living God. As God has said:
'I will dwell in them and walk among them. I will be their
God, and they shall be My people.'"

Throughout scripture, when God is talking about His relationship and interaction with His people, He uses three main prepositions: with, in *and* among. He talks about making His home with us (Jn. 14:23), walking among us (2 Cor. 6:16 / Lev. 26:12), dwelling in us (2 Cor. 6:16), and dwelling among us (Ezek. 37:27). This becomes even more amazing when you understand what these prepositions mean.

With:
...indicate[s] one that shares in an action, transaction, or arrangement
...indicate[s] accompaniment or companionship
...indicate[s] connection or relationship and idea, state, or action
...indicate[s] combination or mixture of ingredients
Joined to
Placed, arranged, or grouped in the same space

Among:
Intermingled with
Surrounded by
In the midst of
In company with

In:
...indicate[s] a position or relationship of authority or responsibility
...indicate[s] close connection by way of implication or active participation
...indicate[s] something that envelops or covers
Under the influence of
...indicate[s] means or instrumentality

Where some of you have thought that God was only inviting you to live a *spiritual* life with Him, He actually invited you to live every aspect of life with Him.

At a fundamental level, God wants the same thing you want when you get into a relationship with someone. When you get into an intimate relationship with another person, you don't get into that relationship to live separate lives that never connect, never intersect.
You don't get into relationship with them to exist as if you barely know each other.
You get into relationship to be with that person,
to do life with them,
to do daily, regular, consistent, ongoing life with them: in the big things, the small things, the mundane things, the exciting things.
You get with them to be involved, connected.
You come into relationship because you're ready for the overlapping of your lives.
You're content with the reality that the more intimate your relationship becomes, the less separate everything about you, as individuals, becomes.

But there are also things that He wants in you,
for you,
through you.

For you, He wants you to be healed, healthy, whole, provided for, living in purpose.
He wants you to have the desires of your heart.
He wants you to experience a fulfilled life in all facets of life.
He wants you to walk through life so secure that there isn't one thing that can separate you from His love.
He wants you secure that there is no limit to where He would go to shower you with that love.
For you, He wants you to know that He has you and He has your life, that He's able to be, and do, anything that you need,
and He wants to be, and do, all that you need.
Because that's what you do for those you love, don't you?

In you, He wants to see you walk in that assurance.

He wants to see you tackle life like the world is your oyster, because it is. I mean, your Daddy owns it all.
He wants you to understand how to walk and prosper in this covenant.
He wants you to be filled with all the fullness of God.
He wants you mature and fruitful.

Through you, He wants you bearing fruit.
He wants you to provide evidence,
to be His walking PSA,
His Yelp review for what's possible in relationship with Him.
He wants you to be His partner in reconciliation.
He wants to be reconciled with all parts of His creation, and you're a key part of making that happen.
He wants you to present yourself as an agent that He can work through: to be His mouthpiece, His arms, His legs. In a nutshell, these are the things that God wants with you, for you, in you, and through you.

As artists in Christ, each of us must learn how to align our expectations for our artistry and career life with God's expectations for relationship with us. By saying yes to His invitation, we agreed to co-create a new life with Him, yielding our *own space, routine, and rhythm to align* with His.

Again, this new life, routine, and rhythm are not created at the expense of your career. In fact, your career is an essential player in how God's desires with, for, in, and through you are attained.

Scenario #2

Last night, I went to this gathering. At the gathering, I met this guy and we hit it off.

I mean *really* hit it off.

And things happened.

Now, here we are, the next morning.

Neither of us were able to sneak out before the other woke up. So, we're stuck here having to face the now-what-moment, after THE moment. Both of us stare off in silence, suffering through an unbearable awkwardness only intensified by the mountain of unanswered questions, and the uncertainty of whether they should even be asked. I decide I'm going to take one for the team and break the silence. I turn to the guy in this unbearable awkwardness and I break the silence with the following: S*o how do you want to handle our finances?*

Consider: What is so absurdly inappropriate about my question at that moment, in this situation?

The question I posed to you was why my question was such an absurd question at that moment, in this situation.

10 What's Going On Here?

Now, be honest, did you imagine the guy answering my question with something along the lines of: *Umm...wow. I don't even know you like that. I don't even know you.*

When discussing the absurdity of my question in our KAI workshop, Matt gave me life with his response. He said my question was inappropriate at that moment because "there was an assumption of too much relational equity. [My] question was inappropriate for the relationship [me and this random guy] currently ha[d]."

His response sounds deep.
And it is.
But it makes total sense. I mean, random guy and I haven't even defined how things would exist between us past this moment. We'd *at least* need that information before we could even begin to think about such a question.

Now, imagine the same scenario, but I'm God and you're random guy. God turns to you and says, *So, let's talk about how we're going to handle your art life.* Think about that. Think about the times God wants to direct our art life and we experience knee-jerk reactions of hesitating, bucking, or questioning why He's trying to get into that space. If we're honest, it's exactly the reason Matt described. We feel that God trying to direct our art life is too intimate a move for the relationship we feel we currently have with Him. Deep inside, this quiet voice responds to Him saying, *But, I don't know you like that, yet.*

Listen family, if you feel like that, it's so ok. There's nothing wrong with you. You're just facing the reality that you don't know God intimately enough to allow Him into that space in your life. That's not bad. It's honest, and an amazing realization that will catapult you forward in your walk with Him when you address it.

This one-night stand scenario is about dynamics in relationship.

What's going on between us?

Before this guy and I could even begin thinking about how we'd tackle things like finances, we have to determine what exists between us now that last night happened. From this point on:
What are we doing?
And, who are we to each other?
These two questions address a situational and interactive dynamic.

So, let's unpack this.

WHAT ARE WE DOING?

Random guy and I had an "event" that transpired between us last night. The next morning, there are some decisions we have to make in order to know our next moves.

Was last night's "event" a one-time thing, and from here we go on with our lives having no desire to see each other again?

Will it lead to a series of encounters, where we occasionally connect for "events," but basically live separate lives.

Will it lead to a no-risk, no-strings-attached exploration to see if there's anything there beyond the "event?"

Or, will this single encounter lead us into a full-fledged, life-long, all-in relationship?

Our decision about what we're doing from this moment forward affects how we address things between us, like finances.

If last night's "event" was just a one-time thing, or if we decide to just occasionally connect for "events," with no other dealings outside of that purpose, the obvious response would seem to be: *Your finances are your business. My finances are mine. Those have nothing to do with what we did with each other, or why we connect. What happened between us does nothing to change how we handled our own finances before the "event."*

But, if we decide that last night's "event" was the first day of the rest of our lives together, the answer to the finance question would be very different.

In the same way, our answer to the *what are we doing* question with God determines how we handle our art life when we interact with Him.

Think about it: You and God had this amazing encounter. He asked you to spend life with Him, and you said 'yes.' That moment was your "event." Now, what is the *morning-after* situation between the two of you? Did you just have a single amazing experience: it was what it was, and now you go on with your separate lives?
Are you two in a friends-with-benefits dynamic, where you reconnect occasionally, but basically have no intertwining of your lives outside of that?
Are you in a non-committal exploration to see if this will work for you? Or, are you two in a full-fledged, life-long, all-in relationship?

How much would you allow Him to lead your art life if you guys just had a single experience?
How much would you allow Him to lead it knowing you two were in a committed, all-in relationship?

Again, we're taking an honest look at the relationship we currently have so we can get to the one we really want.

I'm confident you want to be all-in with God, holding nothing back. I believe you want to totally surrender your art life to Him. But that's going to take some real self-examination about how you're defining the situation between the two of you. You're also going to need to be honest with yourself about how you're interacting with Him, understanding that your definition affects your interaction.

Are you giving Him access?
If not, what's holding you back?

Sometimes, how we *want* to interact with God, and how we *actually* interact with Him, are different. Getting to the all-in with Him takes us being accountable for the fact that we determine the level of intimacy, surrender, and vulnerability we experience with Him. He's already all-in.

God is already committed to total intimacy with you... but life intimacy with you, not just "spiritual" intimacy.

What do I mean?

Would you agree that sexual intimacy is only part of the intimacy possible in an entire relationship; that there are more ways to be intimate in a relationship besides sex?

Then, in the same way, the "spiritual" things we do in relationship with God - like pray and read the word - those are only part of the way we can be intimate with Him.

Look at it like this:
if you're in a situation where the sex is good, but the rest of the interaction between you sucks, like –
you don't talk,
you have nothing in common,

your lives are completely separate,
the only time the two of you are in the same space is during sex, and
outside of sex you have no idea why you'd even speak to this person –

that situation is not a relationship.

That is a series of encounters.

It's a one-night stand encounter.
A friends-with-benefits arrangement.
A booty-call-without-the-follow-up-how-you-doing-call arrangement.

And we can have these same kinds of arrangements with God and
mistake them for a relationship.

Instead of the one-night stand, we have the one-day
stand: Sunday service.

Or, He's just our regular Wednesday / Sunday hook-up. While we're in
service, we're all loving on Him and telling Him how good He is, and
then we don't talk to Him for the rest of the week.
Our friends don't know Him.
Our family has never met Him or even heard of Him.
There are no pictures or evidence of Him anywhere in our lives.

We just hook up, and then we go back to our separate lives.

We actually could see a good thing going on between us, but we only
see Him as worth committing to a moment with, not someone who's
worth us committing to building a life with. These are our times of
prayer and reading the word, that never actually come off the page, out
of our heads, beyond that singular moment into the rest of our daily
living.

This is us never reaching the point where we say I'm all in,
where we're actually applying this stuff,

where we say here are the keys to my house

no, bump that,

let's buy a new place together.
Here are the passwords to all my social media accounts.
Let's get a joint checking account.

No.

Instead, this is: I see you.
I even like spending time with you when we're together.
But...
I'm also totally good if we're not.
And, I'm really okay if we only see each other occasionally.

This is the arrangement where you get the semblance of the emotional connection, but one gets pushed to the side as soon as the other person finds the one to whom they're actually ready to commit.

But God did not invite you to a life of encounters or arrangements.
He wants it all.

He wants the ring,
the keys to the house,
all your passwords,
joint banking,
pictures of the two of you all on the walls in the house,
pictures of you as wallpaper on your cell phone and your computer.
He wants your nose wide open for Him.

That's where He's at. Are you in the same place? If not, what's holding you back?

Whether you realize it or not, you've defined a situational dynamic between you and God. And, you interact with Him based on that definition. And more, your definition determines the degree to which you allow, or deny, Him access to your art life.

Many of us perceive our salvation experience as an encounter, one that we sometimes struggle to know how to respond to, now that it's happened. We know we want to be with God as we live life, but we're not sure how life is to be lived between us. Us receiving Christ, but living in this ambiguity, is like having a one-night stand with a random person, and having to interact with them the next morning. You don't really know how to be around each other. This leads us to deal with God tentatively, as we see our salvation encounter as something having happened for us spiritually, but having no shifting impact on the way we live, or handle the various facets of our life, now that it's happened.

If you want to experience harmony between faith, art, and career, where all three parts are accepted and honored, making room for this all-in relationship is essential. Remember, to honor faith is to honor its whole environment. Just as you cannot say you honor Chinese culture while disrespecting its social customs and laws, you cannot say you honor faith while disregarding the relationship God wants with you, and the principles that govern how things are done within that relationship.

So, I ask you:

What does it look like for you to give God all your passwords, for you and Him to commit to a 30-year mortgage together in your career?

What does it look like for pictures of you and God to be the wallpaper on your cell phone?

What does it mean for God to be more than just a booty call, a one-night stand, or a friend-with-benefits in your career life?

What does intimacy, I mean true intimacy, with Him actually look like in the day-to-day things you do, in the mundane places you go as a professional artist?

What does it look like to be vulnerable with Him, to let Him into those exposed, tender places of your career life and your artistic desires?

Our desire for harmony is revealing. To varying degrees, it reveals our belief that God's desire to lead our art life is too presumptuous for the level of intimacy we currently have. Again, that's not a bad thing. It's honest, and is a beautiful moment in your relationship if you're willing to address it.

So far, our look into the one-night stand scenario has left us with the task to determine what situation we're willing to be in with God. The next look we take into this scenario will task us to determine who we're willing to be to Him.

WHO WE ARE TO EACH OTHER?

In our first look into this scenario, we talked about your "event" being your acceptance of God's invitation to spend life with Him. Now that your "event" has happened, who are you to one another? Remember, your answer to that question impacts the degree to which you allow Him to be involved in your art life.

Again, embracing total honesty, you've already settled for the role you'll play to Him. And, you've already been governing His involvement in your art life based on the role you've settled into playing. But harmony is about coming to one mind *with Him* about your role in the relationship. It's about accepting and honoring the role He invited you into as you go about art and career.

What is that role?

There are a lot of roles that we play to one another in our relationship with God. Some of them include Savior to redeemed, Creator to creation, Visionary to steward, King to ambassador, and Lord to lord. Still, one role is quintessential to our relationship: Father to son.

157

(Let me note very quickly that by son, I'm not speaking to gender, but to disposition. The Greek word is *huios*, meaning "one with the nature and character of." This use of son refers to men and women.)

> Gal. 4:4-6
> "But when the fullness of the time had come, God sent forth His Son, born of a woman, born under the law, to redeem those who were under the law, that we might receive the adoption as sons. And because you are sons, God has sent forth the Spirit of His Son into your hearts, crying out, 'Abba, Father!'"

> 1 Jn. 3:2
> "Beloved, now are we the sons of God, and it doth not yet appear what we shall be: but we know that, when he shall appear, we shall be like him; for we shall see him as he is."

> Eph. 1:5
> "having predestined us to adoption as sons by Jesus Christ to Himself, according to the good pleasure of His will,"

> Rom. 8:29
> "For whom He foreknew, He also predestined *to be* conformed to the image of His Son, that He might be the firstborn among many brethren."

> Rom. 8:19
> "For the earnest expectation of the creation eagerly waits for the revealing of the sons of God."

In these scriptures, we see that our primary role to one another in relationship is that of Father to son, not God to artist. *But wait*, you say, *God made me an artist*. And to that I say, *Yes, He did*.

You *are* an artist.
But you're not *just* an artist.
Nor are you *first* an artist.
You're an artist existing on the other side of a 'yes.'

That 'yes' has re-oriented everything about your existence as an artist. As an artist who has said 'yes,' your artistry is now contained in your sonship.
As one who has said 'yes,' you are a son who expresses your sonship through your artistry.

This is a very important distinction for us to make, particularly those of us who think of ourselves as being artists, who just happen to be Christian.

Why?

As an artist on the other side of a 'yes,' there's an *in you* and *through you* part of being in relationship with God. He is for your art life and career, but in inviting you to relationship, He's after more than you just having a career. Embracing your sonship in your art life is important to the full intention of God's invitation to you.

Now, let's talk about this sonship thing.
What's that about?
Well, it's about position, inheritance, and disposition. But, for the sake of our conversation, we're going to focus on disposition.

Basically, your sonship causes you to regard and manage your art life in a particular way.

> Rom. 8:14
> "For as many as are led by the Spirit of God, these are sons of God."

> Lk. 8:21
> "And it was told Him *by some,* who said, 'Your mother and Your brothers are standing outside, desiring to see You.' But He answered and said to them, 'My mother and My brothers are these who hear the word of God and do it.'"

In Eph. 4:1, we're beseeched to "walk worthy of the calling with which [we've been] called." We've been made, and are called, sons (1 Jn. 3:2). Sons are led by the Spirit of God. Sons make it a priority to hear the word of God on a matter, and do what they've heard Him say in that matter.

So, if you're a son who expresses your sonship through your art life, and a son is one who is led by the Spirit of God, what does this mean for the way you exist as an artist and traverse your career?

Well, most importantly, it means you have a decision to make.

Are you going to walk worthy of the sonship you've been called to in your art life?

Are you going to let God connect you with that director you've always wanted to work with His way? Or, are you going to do it by the means you see everyone else doing it?

Are you going to go to those contract negotiations and say what God told you to say? Or, are you going to follow the advice of your agent?

Are you going to say *no* to that project, like God told you to? Or, are you going to say *yes* because everyone else is telling you that your career won't survive if you say no?

Are you going to make that phone call to the studio owner, like God told you to do? Or, are you not going to call because you don't understand how they'd possibly say yes to what He told you to ask them?

Whose report will you believe?
Whose way will you follow?
Who's going to lead you into the promised land of your career?
Is it going to be you and your own understanding and education?
Is it going to be other people whose careers you're wanting to emulate?

Is it going to be your agent or manager?
Or, is it going to be the Spirit of God?

Scenario #3

Imagine you have two types of friends. The first type is your easy-going, no-fuss friend. You don't have to do much to entertain them. They're self-sufficient. They're the friend that just comes over to be in the same space with you. They tag along with you on your errands to the store. They eat what's already in the house. They watch what's already on TV, or whatever you were planning to watch before they came over. You don't even really have to pay attention to them. You could be doing something in another room and they'd be perfectly fine. Their presence doesn't change anything about what you're doing, or were planning to do before they got there.

Then you have the other kind of friend, your disruptive friend. These are the friends who demand your attention. You have to shift your day to accommodate them. These friends aren't going to be okay with just sitting in your house while you do chores, or running errands with you. These are the friends who want you to abandon that laundry you were about to do, and instead, get dressed up and go somewhere. They're the ones that come in and shift the environment of your space. They call you and ask you what you're doing today, but they don't really care because they already have something planned for you guys. Every time they call, you know whatever you intended to do is thrown out the window.

Consider: What possible issues could arise by not understanding which friend you're dealing with?

11 Who've you Let into your House?

In this scenario, we looked at two types of friends. I asked you what potential problems could arise by not understanding the friend with whom you were dealing.

This scenario is about properly relating to the Person we've invited to take residence in our life. As I'm sure you've guessed, Christ is the second friend (the disruptive one). While we can easily and immediately recognize this in the scenario, we, all too often, forget it when we interact with Him in real life.

Because we misunderstand the type of person with whom we're engaged, we struggle to properly orient our art life in our relationship with Him.
Is He just along for the ride while we go about our business as career artists?
Or does He have expectations of His own that He's brought into the relationship?
And, how are we supposed to respond to those expectations?
Harmony between faith, art, and career can't be experienced if you don't understand who you've let into your house.

So, who have we let into our house?

> Philippians 2:9-11
> "Therefore God also has highly exalted Him and given Him the name which is above every name, that at the name of Jesus every knee should bow, of those in heaven, and of those on earth, and of those under the earth, and that every tongue should confess that Jesus Christ is Lord, to the glory of God the Father."

When we gave our life to God at salvation, our declaration was that we were embracing His Lordship in our lives. We tend to miss this. We have no problem engaging with the Savior part of Christ, but we struggle submitting to the Lord part of Christ. Yet, in Philippians 2, we clearly see that the confession that leads to salvation is that Christ is Lord, not Savior.

Why is this difference so important? Let's answer that by first looking at Luke 6:46:

> "But why do you call Me 'Lord, Lord,' and not do the things which I say?"

Your relationship with God has always been about Him being Lord in your life, from the very beginning. The whole point of your relationship, from its start, was that you, from this moment forward, would allow Him to lead you into the life He designed for you. That is, and has always been, the whole point of your coming together. However, even though He is Lord *to* you, He isn't interested in lording *over* you - which is why His lordship in your life is housed within His relationship to you as Father. He leads you as Lord, but He does so in the spirit of a loving father who wants what's best for you, and who wants to care for you. He doesn't lord over you as one who's ready to punish you, humiliate you, take from you, and cause you suffering.

What does all this mean for building harmony between faith, art, and career?

We've established that, as artists on the other side of a 'yes,' we are sons who express our sonship through our art life. That means we're artists who submit to God as He leads us in creating art, managing our career, and interacting with others.

But, in our one-night stand scenario, we uncovered a source of hesitancy, where we struggle to allow God to be Lord in our art life because we don't feel that we know Him intimately enough to be comfortable with Him in that place. This impacts our ability to fully live as the sons God empowered us to be.

I was talking to my friend, Tawanna, about the evolution of our intimacy with God. Before we come into relationship with Him, we see Him as *God, over there*. Then we get saved and initially begin to know Him as friend, who cares about us. As we grow in intimacy, we get to know Him as Father, who takes care of us. And only then, when we know He cares about us and we've experienced Him caring for us, can we allow ourselves to interact with Him as Lord. Relating to Him as Lord is the deepest level of trust and intimacy we could have with Him, where we give Him the ability to make critical decisions over the most precious, sacred parts of our life.

This degree of intimacy requires compromise. It requires a willingness to let go of plans, perceptions, and timetables. It requires an openness to rearranging, restructuring, reframing, and indirect routing. It requires the relinquishing of the thing many of us are most afraid to let go of: control.
And all of that requires trust.

I was talking to a video cohort of KAI participants in New York. In one of the sessions, we dealt with this issue of trust where I led them through a series of questions. The first question that I had them answer for themselves was, *what does it mean to trust someone?*

One of the ladies said it was about fully believing the other person has your best interest at heart. It was about having the confidence that you could put your life in their hands and be safe.

So, I asked her, "Do you believe that God has your best interest at heart?"
She smiled, and said, "Yes."

Then I asked her, "Do you trust that your life is safe in God's hands?"
She smiled, again, and said, "Yes."

Then I asked her, "If that's the case, why is it still so difficult for you to trust Him with your career? Why do you struggle to fully put your career in His hands, and allow it to be fully led and directed by Him?" And, again, she smiled, but this time with one of those *DANG* faces.

She had to pause and think about that one. We all have to pause and think about this.
Because these are the things that we say.
These are the things that effortlessly fly out of our mouths.

Yes, I love God!
Ok.

And we say, *Yes, I trust God!*
But in this conversation I just shared with you, we see that saying we trust God and walking in trust are two different things.

If you're going to experience harmony between your faith, art, and career, you're going to have to allow God to lead you. In order to let Him lead you, you're going to have to allow yourself to develop trust in Him. But, you won't trust God if you don't settle some things within yourself about the God who's asking for your trust.

I, myself, am a career artist. I'm a choreographer and teacher. Even though I've written this book and developed the Kingdom Artist Initiative (KAI), I still have desires as an artist. I want to continue producing work regionally through my company, Speak Hill Dance Project. I also want to do freelance work, setting pieces on major companies. And I was well on my way. I started my dance company and produced my first show. I was showcasing work in festivals and getting good feedback. Opportunities were starting to come in regularly. Relationships were being built. Collaborations were being set up. Things were beginning to roll quite nicely...finally. Then God said *I need you to put your choreography work down and build KAI.*

Huh!?

So, I've laid my company life down for this season to develop KAI, but the biggest thing I had to do was trust God enough *to* lay it down. Now, I haven't completely abandoned my artistry. I still teach occasionally. I still go to see shows. I still take classes. I still write down the names of dancers with whom I want to work. I still network. I still research choreography opportunities so I'll be ready when God releases me. I still make small phrases and record them. But, for this season, I've been asked to direct my energy to building KAI, instead of building dances.

And that requires tremendous trust. TREMENDOUS trust!

I have to trust Him when He says that if I lose my life for His sake, I'll find it.
I have to trust Him when He says He'll give me the desires of my heart.
I have to trust that if I lay my career down, and follow Him where He's asking me to go, that He'll honor His word in my life.
I have to trust Him beyond my own fears of *what if they don't remember me, what if my window passes, what if He never releases me to be a choreographer again.*
I have to trust Him that He'll redeem the time, the progress, and the momentum that it seems like I'm losing by not being out there making and presenting work. What if they forget about me? What if I lose my edge? Will my ability as a choreographer diminish because I haven't been using it?

These are all fears that I have constant opportunity to give in to.
Instead, I choose to trust Him, to do what He's asked of me - taking off my choreographer hat and putting on my developing hat for a season.

My life is walking this whole trust line. So, believe me when I tell you that I understand where and how this is difficult for you.
I've walked away from jobs.
I've moved to another city with no money or relationships in the new place.
I've launched out full throttle into projects when I had no idea how to pay for them.
I've developed the confidence to release and tackle things at His word.

How am I able to walk in this kind of abandon with God? And how will you be able to do it?

First, let's talk about how trust is developed, because we often misunderstand how we grow in it.

Most of us want to trust God more, but we think about trust like we think about baking a cake: When I get the ingredients, I'll bake the cake. In the same way, we pray to God for more trust, thinking that He'll give us more trust and then we'll use the trust He just gave us to trust Him more.

But that's not how trust is matured and increased.

Trust is a product. By that, I mean that it's the result of some previous action.
It starts as risk and ends as trust.

At some point, you're going to have to take a risk and try something that He's led you to do, even though you don't have the absolute certainty you desire.
Then, as you move out on what He's led you to do,
and you experience His response to your obedience,
and you experience His response to your willingness to believe Him,
when you experience Him show up for you and come through for you,
what results is that you trust Him a little more for the next time He leads you to do something.
The next time you step out on His word, you experience the same, and a little more trust is developed. And so on, and so on. This continues with Him gradually asking you to step out and believe Him in bigger things, until you get to a point where He has come through enough, and been so faithful, that there's no place you wouldn't follow Him.

Now, what gets you to the place where you're willing to take that step? Like I said in the beginning, you can't do this until you know the person asking you to do it. I don't mean you know who He *is*, I mean you know *Him*. Then you have to believe some things about Him.

What am I talking about?

The most important thing to remember is who's asking for your trust.

So, who's asking?

It's not enough to just know God is asking. That's important. That's very important, but still not close to your everyday life. That's why you can know it's Him asking, that He loves you, and still hold your daily life very distant from Him.

We know it's Him asking, but who is *He*?

He's the God who put the gift in you in the first place.
He's the God who activated the itch in you to pursue a career in mainstream culture.
He's the God who says, *I plant you, My child, as seed in this world. You're out there because I've led you there, planted you there. So, no, your career doesn't dishonor or offend Me. You're not out of My will, or disobeying My word, by being "out there" because I have you there for a reason. Why would I activate a desire in you to want this, and then tell you that you can't have it? I'm asking you to let Me put my hands in your art career - not to take it from you, but to walk with you, to support you in making sure it becomes all I've purposed it to be. I am after something bigger, in you and through you, than just your career as an artist. I need you to have a career as an artist. I take pleasure in you having a career as an artist. But that's not all I'm after.*

This is the God who's asking for our trust.

And, knowing this about Him is what makes me willing to lay down my choreography hat for a season. But that's not enough.
That makes me *willing* to do it.
What makes me *actually* do it?

To actually do it, there are some things I have to believe about Him, and that you're going to have to believe about Him.

One: You're going to have to believe that He knows what you want, which we established. He knows what you want because He put it in you to want it.

Two: You have to believe that He wants for you what you want. Your "secular" art career is not offensive to Him. He put you there, so He wants you to be there.

Three: You have to believe that He's able to get you what you want. It's one thing for Him to know what you want, and to want *for you* what you want. That will give you some sense of comfort and support. But, then, you also have to believe that He has the capacity and the ability to actually get you into it.

For me, I have to believe that if I follow what He's leading me to do, instead of following industry advice, that He can back up what He's said. My career as a choreographer means a lot to me. He's asked me to trust Him with something for which I've made a lot of sacrifice. I personally fought for 12 years to get into a dance program and went through a lot of painful stuff to get to this point. Many of you can relate to this.

Your art career is something that you dream about day and night, and pursue with your whole heart. Some of you have moved from other states,
left your families,
almost went homeless (some of you have actually been homeless),
worked seven weird jobs at a time just to create space to go on auditions and be ready when your time came.
You've looked stupid and irresponsible in front of people, daring to believe that you could actually make a go of this. You've done all this, and then Jesus comes along and asks you to put it all in His hands. Like me, you need to feel confident that He knows what He's doing.

I mean, would you let your grandmother be your agent and negotiate a $100 million movie deal for you?

No!

Why?

Because she doesn't know what she's talking about, even though she knows you want to be in film and she wants you to be in film. It's not enough for you to know that God wants you in culture. You have to trust that He's able to help you be successful there; or else you won't follow His guidance. Instead, you'll follow the one you feel is most capable of helping you be successful in what you're trying to accomplish.

Four: You have to believe that He's willing to help you get what you want, and that He'll actually get in it with you.

I could look at you and say, *I know you want some money to go on this retreat. And, I want you to have the money to go on the retreat, because I want you to have the experience.*

I'm even able to give you the money so you can go. I have it right now.

However, with all that, it doesn't mean that I'm actually *willing* to give you the money, even though I have the money, I want you to have the experience, and I know this is something you really want to do.

So, you also have to believe that He has determined to journey with you until you get it.

In a KAI workshop session, we were going over this and one participant asked, "We've been talking about God getting us what we want. Shouldn't we be focused on what God wants?"

That was such a great question. Yes, we should be focused on what God wants. I reminded her that we were operating on the premise that this career life *is* among what God has for us. Again, this is a conversation to artists who sense a holy drawing to an art career in "secular" culture, yet struggle with confidence, lack know-how, or need support to stand flat-footed and know God is for them being there, and is there with them. This belief conversation is still important, even under such a premise, because we can believe God is drawing us to such a career life and still struggle to allow Him to lead us in it. This belief conversation is about getting to the place where we feel safe enough to open ourselves up to experiences with God, which will build up our trust in Him.

Where do you start in allowing Him to be Lord in your art life? You have to do like Mufasa told Simba: REMEMBER!

One of the things that God was always getting on the children of Israel about, besides their nut-crazy disobedience, was not to forget. He brought them out of Egypt to possess the land He had for them, and to live with them in community as their God.
But that was going to take a lot of feats of faith.
So, He was always encouraging them to remember what He'd done before, because that would help them muster up the courage to do the next crazy thing He'd lead them to do. Inevitably, they *would* forget and act 'brand new,' like they had no idea that God wanted to, or was able to, bring them all the way into their promised land.

In Deut. 7:18 and 11:7, He tells the children of Israel to remember what they saw Him do. In chapter 11, He tells them to make sure to keep His commandments *because* of what they've seen Him do. Remembering what God has done in your life will help you in the same way.

So, here's what I want you to do:
I want you to think back on all the prayers over your art career that God answered,
all the times He made a way for you,
all the times He gave you favor,
all the times you achieved something that you know couldn't have been done unless He stepped in.

Put them all in a list.

Then I want you to make copies of that list and post them where you spend a lot of time. Every time you pray, especially when you pray about your career, I want you to have that list.

And then, I want you to start saying out of your own mouth *God I trust you. I trust you because you've proven time and time again that I am safe with you, and that my art career is safe with you.*

When He leads you to do something, look at that list, and take a risk on the One who's been consistently faithful to you. As you do that, trust is being built. Eventually, it'll just be second nature.

Scenario #4

Imagine there's this person that you find really attractive at your job. You guys have been orbiting around each other for some time. You're definitely on one another's radar, but nothing has happened yet. No defining moment has happened to shift the dynamic between the two of you. Then one day something does happen. And it's an amazing experience. But, it's not a definitively situation-changing experience. The next day at work, things between you are charged, but ambiguous; leaving you unclear about how to act around each other.

Consider: Why don't you know how to act around one another? Why is it so hard for you to know what to do next? What would help you know what to do next?

12 **Happened, but Undefined**

In this scenario, we explored a workplace attraction between you and a co-worker, where you had an amazing experience with one another, but didn't know how to interact the next day at work. We called the situation between you "charged, but ambiguous." The questions I posed in this scenario were:

Why don't you know how to act around one another?

Why is it so hard for you to know what to do next?

What would help you know what to do next?

There's one thing that makes the situation between the two of you hairy: the ambiguity. You know you guys had an amazing time together. You know this amazing time *could* have changed things between you. But you're unsure if it's *actually* changed things between you. And if it has, you don't know what it's changed, or what you're supposed to do around each other in the change. This same ambiguity exists in our relationship with God, and it impacts our ability to experience harmony between our faith, art, and career.

Becoming a part of the body of Christ has changed your art life.

When it comes to our faith life, we recognize that something happened. However, we don't always recognize that things have changed because of what happened. More specifically, we don't understand *how* things have changed, or how we're to orient our life to cooperate with the change. Part of experiencing harmony is recognizing that becoming a part of the body of Christ has changed your art life. And, honoring faith in your art life means cooperating with that change in the way you engage in its creative, business, and social facets.

Ok, so what's the change, and how do you cooperate with it as a career artist?

The change
When you got saved, you became a new creation (2 Cor. 5:17),
were made a citizen of a new kingdom (Col. 1:13),
and you were made accountable to a new system (Rom. 1:17).
This new system is governed by different laws,
it upholds different standards and values,
practices different customs,
and has a different way of getting things done.

Cooperating with this change means managing the creative, business, and social parts of your art life as it's now done in the new system you've come into. So, how are things done in this new system?

The new way
> Rom. 1:17
> "For in it the righteousness of God is revealed from faith to faith; as it is written, 'The just shall live by faith.'"

The just shall live by faith. As artists in Christ, we're part of the just. This means we also have to live by faith, even in our art life. What does this mean?

Let's answer that by looking at the word *by*. It's easy to bypass this word, assuming it's insignificant in this sentence. But, it was actually the word God used to explain this verse to me.

By:
The means of achieving something
Through the work or operation of
In conformity or harmony with

Let's see what that shows us:

The just shall live by the working of faith.
The just shall conform their activity to the way faith operates.
The just achieve things by putting their faith into operation.

In the Kingdom of God, faith is the way things move and are accomplished. And faith is honored in our art and career when we work faith in them. Now, what does the working of faith look like? For our conversation, we find the answer in 2 Cor. 4:13 and James 2:18.

It's in your mouth.
2 Cor. 4:13 "Yet we have the same spirit of faith as he had who wrote, I have believed, and therefore have I spoken. We, too, believe, and therefore we speak."

The first way you work faith is to speak what you believe. 2 Cor. 4:13 tells us that people with the spirit, or the mindset, of faith function this way: They speak what they believe. Mk. 11:23 tells us we'll have whatever we say. You and I were created in the image and likeness of a Creator who spoke His world into existence. He created all things by His word (Heb. 11:3). As one made to function like Him, you, too, are to participate in bringing your artistic dreams into existence by speaking to them, over them, and about them.

So, here's the question you have to consider:
What have you been speaking over your art life?
What have you been saying about your creativity,
about your art pieces,
about your access to opportunities,
about the pace of your career progress,

about your place in your industry and artform,
about your status among peers,
about your place at the table?

Have you been saying what God has shown and said to you?
Have you been speaking life into the things you're believing Him to do
for you?
Or, have you been reporting and echoing what you see, and spouting
off how you feel in the moment?

Here's an even deeper question for you: What do you believe?
We speak what we believe, so what do you believe?
Do you believe what God has said about your art career?
Do you even know what He's said about it?
If you don't know what He's said about your career, or who you are as
an artist, how can you believe Him about it? And, if you don't know
what *He's* said, what have you been exercising belief in?

You can tell what you've believed by what you've been speaking and
doing. You can tell by the things that've been leading your decision
making in your art career.

Faith speaks what it believes; not what it sees, and not what it feels.
This is really important for you to assess because the art life you have
now is partly a product of what you've been saying about it. Honoring
faith in the way you do your art and career means working faith in the
way you do art and career – which we now know includes speaking into
it. If you want what God has for you, you have to make sure you're
echoing the things He's sharing, and speaking those things you're
believing to happen. As I was taught, you have to make sure the things
you're saying over an area match what you're praying about it.

Why is this important?

In Jer. 1:12, God says He watches over His word to perform it— that's
anywhere His word is spoken, anywhere it's regarded and cooperated

with. If you want God to move in your career life, you have to start at His word, because that's where He starts.

Another part of this speaking practice is that we're to speak about things God has said like they already exist, before we can actually see them (Rom. 4:17). We do this because they do exist, just not in a form we can perceive, yet. We see God do this with Abram and Sarai. In Gen. 12, He tells Abram that He'll make him into a great nation. In Gen. 15, He tells him that his offspring will be as numerous as the stars. In Gen. 17, God tells Abram He'll multiply him exceedingly. Then, working faith, He changes Abram and Sarai's name to correspond with the promise He gave them. Abram's name was changed to Abraham, meaning *father of many nations,* or *father of a multitude.* And He changed Sarai's name to Sarah, as a *mother of nations.*

They had no children at the time God changed how He referred to them.
And God didn't wait until after they had children to change it.
He started speaking over them according to what He promised. And He made it so that they would speak about each other according to what He promised them.
He did this before anything ever happened.
As those made in His image and likeness, we're to cooperate with His promises to us in the same way.

In practicing this, one of the things that was difficult for me to navigate was how to speak about my current situation without lying, and without speaking against what I was believing to happen, but hadn't happened yet.

Col. 4:6 says, *"Let* your speech always *be* with grace, seasoned with salt, that you may know how you ought to answer each one." Part of your speech being with grace is letting the Spirit of God lead and influence what comes out of your mouth.

One example I have of this practice is when I wanted to speak to someone about helping me, while explaining to them that I didn't have a lot of money. The Lord had gotten on me about saying I didn't have money, even though, technically, it was absolutely the truth. I struggled to know how to say it. I wanted to let the person know that I didn't have a lot of money because I needed to know if he'd be willing to help me even though I didn't have money. I mean, how would he know unless I told him? But, I also wanted to be obedient by not saying I didn't have money. Also, I didn't want to perpetuate not having money by continuing to say I didn't have it. So, what did I do? I asked the Holy Spirit how I should say it, and He told me how to say it. I explained it by saying I was in a season of financial transition.

In the same way, I encourage you to ask God how to speak about your art, career, and industry relationships so that you remain in the language of faith, without lying or speaking against the things you're believing Him for.

To the brim
2 Cor. 4:13 tells us that people in the mindset of faith speak what they believe. Lk. 6:45 gives us another nugget, telling us that people speak out of the abundance of their heart. This tells us that if we want to speak what God has said, we have to get full of what He's saying. How do we do that?

One way to get full of what God is saying is to consume it until you're full. God's word comes to us by Scripture. We need to spend time in Scripture. It's the foundation of His communication with us. In it, we find His promises to us and instruction on how to obtain them in our lives (2 Tim. 3:16-17). God also speaks to us by His inspired, or proceeding word. Mt. 4:4 tells us we're to live by this proceeding word. This is daily guidance, instruction, and inspiration that come from the Spirit of God to lead us in a more hands-on, step-by-step fashion.

Another way to get full is to steep in it.

Josh. 1:8
"This Book of the Law shall not depart from your mouth,
but you shall meditate in it day and night, that you may
observe to do according to all that is written in it. For then
you will make your way prosperous, and then you will have
good success."

One KAI participant, Steven, used the word *marinate*, which I really like. If you've ever marinated meat, you know that the flavors begin to transfer into the meat as it sits in the marinade. Likewise, you get full of God's Word by steeping in it, letting Him unpack what He's said to you, mulling over the things He's showing you, communing with Him over the things He's ministering to you about your art life. As you meditate on what He's said, He begins to give you specific direction and instruction to bring those things to pass in your life.

So, the first way to work faith is to speak it. The second way is by action.

Show Me

James 2:18
"But someone will say, 'You have faith, and I have works.'
Show me your faith without your works, and I will show
you my faith by my works."

Just like faith is worked by speaking what you believe, it's also worked by taking action according to what you believe. What does this look like?

Let's say you were believing God to present a short film at Sundance. You pray about it, He gives you the go-ahead, and you begin speaking faith over your spot in the festival. That's fantastic! Now, what are you *doing* to get into Sundance? How are your actions putting faith to work? Are you taking film classes?
Are you getting feedback on your film to get it as sharp as possible before you submit it?

Are you out networking to meet potential collaborators? You can't make the film on your own.
Have you researched how to apply to Sundance?
Do you know the application deadlines and festival dates?
Do you know which category you want to apply for?
Have you made the film?
Have you finished the script?
What are you doing about what God has said?
How are you preparing to receive what you've asked Him for?

Faith is worked by acting on what God has shared, or what you're believing Him to do in your art and career. But, working faith in your art life is difficult if you can't remember what's been shown or communicated. So, I encourage you to follow His instruction to Habbakuk:

> Habakkuk 2:2-3
> "Then the LORD answered me and said:
> 'Write the vision
> And make *it* plain on tablets,
> That he may run who reads it.
> For the vision *is* yet for an appointed time;
> But at the end it will speak, and it will not lie.
> Though it tarries, wait for it;
> Because it will surely come,
> It will not tarry.'"

Write it down!
Write it down so you can remember it.
Write it down so you can speak it.
Write it down so you can check it off when God keeps His word about it.
Write it down so you can go back and see how He's been faithful and kept His word.
Write it down so you can run!

Now, this all sounds good. But, what does it look like in actual practice?

In 2011, I was in my third year of teaching at the performing arts high school. And I was loving it! One day, I was standing out in the hall during a passing period. I loved doing this because I got to chat with my students, give them hugs, joke around, etc. I was standing there watching them, and out of nowhere, the Lord said, "Four years. In four years, it will be time to go." That's literally all He said. I went and wrote it down, dated it, and went on about my business. Two months after that, my pastor prophesied over me, saying, "In about four years, the Lord [would] begin to call [me] to different places—particularly to Europe." I ran and wrote that down, and went on about my business.

Now, I didn't know anyone in Europe.
I wasn't thinking about Europe.
Didn't know how I was going to get to Europe.
And, I didn't start trying to figure out how to get to Europe.
I just lifted it up in prayer and thanked God for His word coming to pass in my life. I didn't receive any further instruction, so I continued focusing on being a great teacher at the high school.

I heard nothing about this again until 2015.

In 2015, I had just published the second edition of my first book. One day, the Lord led me to an excerpt from it.
He told me to narrate it.
He told me what song to use behind the narration.
And, He told me to go into the studio, make a dance to it, and record it. Then He told me to start reaching out to other people in the faith and art community and, when I did, to attach my video in the email.

That was the only instruction He gave me. So that's what I did.

The first person I reached out to was a guy who was hosting a workshop for his arts ministry. I emailed him on a Wednesday. It was February 4th, 2015. What I didn't know was that he, and this other woman, were supposed to do a chapel at Biola University on that Friday. He's a visual artist. She's a storyteller. And they were supposed to do this chapel with a dancer. But, the dancer had to drop out for some reason. So, they were looking for a dancer when I sent him my email with my video attached.

He showed my email to the storyteller and she told him to ask me if I was available. He emailed me back and invited me to do the chapel with them. I didn't know these people, but I felt led to say yes. So, I did.

I show up to the chapel.
I meet them for the first time.
We do the chapel.
It's a God connection.

Afterwards, I got to talk more with the woman. Our vendor tables were right next to each other. In talking to her, I found out that she runs this organization, Edge Project, that takes a group of artists to Spain every summer. I noted it, but didn't feel led to say, or do, anything about it. I didn't tell her anything about what God had said to me.

Over the next year, we talked two, maybe three, times. I didn't pursue her. I didn't feel led to research her organization. And God hadn't given me any other instruction about Europe. I just kept going to work, kept writing, kept making dances and doing whatever else I felt led to tackle.

Then one day, she invites me down to San Diego where she asks me if I would pray about being part of the Edge team in Spain. I remember asking her, "Is Spain in Europe?" I knew that Spain was in Europe, but I was making a point. She looked at me curiously and answered, "Yes." I smiled and said, "Well, then I don't have to pray about that. I know what God said. I'll be there." My last day at the school was on Monday, June 13, 2016. The very next day, I was on a plane to Spain.
I didn't do anything else to try to get to Europe.
I would've never guessed that sending that email would land me in Europe.
I didn't know who these people were.

I just heard God tell me to make a video and include it in my emails to people in the faith and art community. And that's what I did.

He led me into what He said He would do for me.

He provided for what He was doing for me.

I just needed to hear and follow.

And that's all you'll need to do to walk in the fullness of what He has for you.

Well, there you have it!

I know we've talked about a whole lot of things over the course of this conversation; but they've all only been about one thing: liberating you to seize the art life God has for you, without apology.

In Closing

Specifically, we set out to free you to be unapologetic about the kind of art you make, where you make it, and who you make it with. For a Christian forging an art career in "secular" culture, that freedom comes through knowing two things:
1 that such an art career is a valid way to participate in Kingdom citizenship and Christian community, which we established in the Liberty section, and
2 that God is for such a career and is in it with you, which we established in the Harmony section.

You don't have to continue in discord because you're exactly where you need to be.
You're in relationship with God because He initiated the relationship.
You have artistic gifts and inclinations because that's how He built you.
You create the kind of art you create about the kind of subjects you explore because that's where He inspires you.
And, you're compelled to a career in "secular" culture because that's the context into which He's drawn you.

God and His kingdom are served, built, honored, and represented in your art life, and by it, even though your language and subject matter don't focus on them:
By the artist you determine to be,
By the way you create art, make career decisions, and interact with those you encounter throughout your career, and
By the way you explore the subjects you tackle in your art.
It's safe for your faith, art, and career to work harmoniously together.

Yes, there are presumptive views about what a Christian's art life should look like. And I know you've been hesitant about them being in the same space. But we've addressed that.

You will not lose, be kept out of, or miss out on any part of what God has planted in your spirit about your career if you follow His leading into it. You won't have to compromise your faith for your artistry, or your artistry for your faith. With God at the helm, there is purpose, reciprocity, and freedom found in bringing faith, art, and career together.

There's tremendous sense of purpose and fulfillment found when your art life is grounded in your relationship with Him.

There's reciprocity between them. They feed each other. They equip each other. They nourish each other. They ground each other.

And, there's freedom. There is such great freedom in walking with God in your art life.

There's no one way for us to serve God.
There's no one look for the Christian's art life.
We will look different.
We exist in different contexts,
which calls for different ways of engaging.
But it's the same God at work in each of us.
We're all serving the same God, working on the same mission.

Therefore, there's nothing in your art life that needs to be apologized for.
God made you an artist.
He's with you as an artist.
And, He's proud of the artist you are, even in your kind of art life.

So be free.

With conscience clean, heart rooted, do your art.
Be the artist God is drawing you to be.

No apology necessary.

Just the beginning

Thank you so much for reading **Defying Discord**. I pray that you feel encouraged and liberated. In that, this book is only meant to be the first part of a larger conversation and relationship. I want to continue journeying with you in ending the divide between your faith and "secular" art career so that you can unapologetically build a Spirit-led art life that contributes to the Kingdom, the community, and the artform.

Here are some ways for us to continue journeying together:
- Connect with our reader community on Facebook. This is where I get to engage with readers. Ask me questions, share your thoughts, and post your favorite parts.
Defying Discord Reader Community: facebook.com/defyingdiscord

- Tune in to our podcast, The Kingdom Art Life.
On iTunes or at thekingdomartlife.com

- Attend one of our KAI webinars, intensives, or prayer collectives.
Find scheduling info at marlitahill.com or fb/iammarlitahill

- Invite me as a speaker for your event or gathering.

- Join our mailing list to receive new content and info about events.
Web: marlitahill.com
FB/IG: @iammarlitahill

Help us Spread the Liberty

Are you excited about this work and think other artists would be encouraged by reading it? **Become a Liberty Ambassador** and help us liberate other artists to do the art God is leading them to do, without apology!

Here's how you can help:
- Leave a review on our Amazon product page and/or on our FB Reader Community page at **fb/defyingdiscord**. And share it!!

- Take a picture of yourself with the **Defying Discord** book and share your favorite quote or why you think your friends should read it. Use the hashtag **#defyingdiscord** and link to our Reader Community page.

- Visit our Ambassador page and share on of our images or quotes **marlitahill.com/ambassador**

- Direct friends to our FB Reader Community so they can learn more about the work.

Thanks in advance!!

About the Author

Marlita Hill is a choreographer, author, and speaker. She founded the Kingdom Artist Initiative (KAI), which teaches artists how their faith and art thrive together in church ministry and career life. She has authored three books on the relationship between faith and art, including her latest, Defying Discord, which explores how the "secular" art career serves, builds and represents the Kingdom (January 2018).

In addition to her writing, Hill produces a weekly podcast, The Kingdom Art Life, hosts the Artist Prayer Collective, in partnership with The Salvation Army Hollywood, and serves as the Associate Director for Edge Project, a missions organization focused on art, culture, and faith.

Web: marlitahill.com
FB/IG: @iammarlitahill